The Visitors' Book

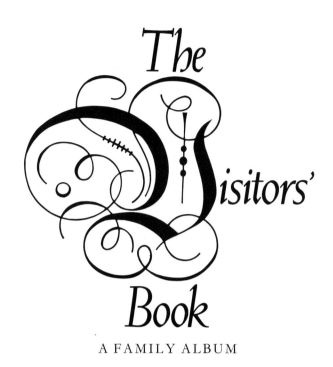

Book

A FAMILY ALBUM

The Visitors' Book

A FAMILY ALBUM

Christopher Simon Sykes

G.P. Putnam's Sons
New York

First American Edition 1978
Copyright © 1978 by Christopher Simon Sykes

First published in Great Britain by
Weidenfeld and Nicolson
11 St John's Hill, London SW11

Designed by Max Fairbrother

Endpapers copyright © 1978 Douglas Cockerell & Son

Library of Congress Catalog Card Number: 78-53402
SBN: 399-12212-5

Filmset and printed in Great Britain by
BAS Printers Limited, Over Wallop, Hampshire

Contents

TO MY FATHER,

MY BROTHERS AND SISTERS,

AND TO THE MEMORY OF MY MOTHER,

WHO I KNOW

WOULD HAVE LAUGHED

Acknowledgments

URING THE PREPARATION of this book I have received assistance from many different directions, and I would like to take this opportunity to thank all those people who have so helped me. In the first place I must express my gratitude to my father for allowing me the use of all the material from Sledmere which is reproduced in the book, and to my brother Tatton for the family trees which he so laboriously drew up for me – particularly as I have been unable to use them!

Although most of the material in this album comes from Sledmere itself, it was occasionally necessary to draw on some outside sources. For these I am indebted equally to the following people: to Bill Cavendish-Bentinck for the loan of Aunt Venetia's photograph albums, and to Joseph and Tina Hoare for her Visitors' books; to the Marquis of Anglesey for his whole-hearted co-operation in providing the sensational photographs of the Dancing Marquis; to Jean Morris for being so kind in parting with the precious albums of her grandfather, Henry Thelwell; to Lady Cavan for lending me the scrapbooks of her father, Henry Cholmondeley; to Liz Walker, whose small album containing early photographs of Sledmere was entrusted to me; and, for various photographs of their ancestors, to Arthur Sygrove, Tom Beacroft, Marion Marshall, and Edie Barr.

In addition my heartfelt thanks are extended to Robert Strickland-Constable for the loan of Great Great Uncle Christopher's fascinating diaries, previously unseen, and to Kitty Thomas for the manuscript of Peter Mellini's new book on her father, Sir Eldon Gorst, *The Overshadowed Proconsul*, which gave me a new insight into Jessica's downfall. For furnishing me with all kinds of family anecdotes I am equally grateful to Archie Hunter, Barbara Cavendish-Bentinck, Denise Ebury, Lydia Bedford, Edward James, Freya Elwes, and Angela Antrim. Angela Antrim also deserves a special tribute for her superb caricatures of my ancestors at the beginning of the book, and which incidentally provide an interesting comparison with those of her father which appear in Chapter 6.

During the writing of the book I have also relied for information on, and occasionally quoted from, the works of my uncle, Christopher Sykes (*Four Studies in Loyalty*, Collins, 1946; *Explorations*, Barrie and Rockliff, 1967) and Professor Roger Adelson (*Portrait of an Amateur*, Jonathan Cape, 1975). Without these my task would have been much harder.

Finally a special thank-you to Annabel Bartlett for reading the manuscript and providing valuable comment, to Max Fairbrother for his hard and diligent work on the design, and to Ed Victor, without whom there might never have been a book at all.

The photographs on pp. 138 and 139 (inset) appear by kind permission of the Radio Times Hulton Picture Library.

Introduction

WHEN I WAS A CHILD there lived in a room at the back of the house, a lady who had been governess to my father. Her name was Mouzelle and to me, and to my sisters and brothers, she seemed at least a hundred years old. 'You are purple with age,' we used to tell her.

Her room was a children's paradise. It was a large, dark, oak-panelled room, incredibly messy, smelly and littered with decaying sofas and chairs, each holding one of my father's numerous greyhounds, who were used to making the place their kennel. Its contents also included a huge and overcrowded roll-top desk; a stereoscope with endless views of the First World War; a hand-cranked film viewer on which we used to watch a girl eating porridge, or a ride on a big dipper; and in one corner, hanging on a screen, Mouzelle's hat and coat, which when put on by any one of us would drive the dogs into a frenzy of barking. This was because they immediately took the wearer to be Mouzelle about to take them for a walk.

At the centre of all this chaos was Mouzelle herself, a frail old lady of Luxembourg origins who used to hold us spellbound with wonderful stories which she related in a rich accent. These 'Mouzelle stories', as they came to be known in the family, were usually about various ancestors and relations, and were repeated over and over again until they were imprinted on the brain (long since her death I have never forgotten them). Although the stories were often questioned – how could anyone wear *six* overcoats? – they were invariably believed in the end, and they sowed in me the seeds of an interest in the more bizarre aspects of my family's history.

This interest needed little encouragement, but there was one final discovery about my family which I was to make, and which led, almost irresistibly, to the creation of this book. This was the unearthing of a unique collection of family photographs. Over the years, my passion for family history had led me to rummage about endlessly in the deep recesses of our house, and these photographs gradually came to light during the many happy hours I spent on these researches. The chest in the library, which I had often noticed but, until that moment, never dared open, its lid bearing the weight of some priceless Ming vase, turned out to be filled almost to overflowing with photographs. In the attics, which I had always steered well clear of as a child for fear of ghosts, trunks thick with dust, and which appeared to contain nothing but reams of dull papers, revealed piles of ancient albums hidden in their depths; while down in the darkest corners of the cellars I found rotting boxes filled with glass lantern slides. Finally, after gathering and sorting all the material, I was able to stand and look down at my Great Great Grandpapa, born in the middle of the eighteenth century, staring arrogantly back at me from his chair, together with all his descendants right up to my father and mother, aunts and uncles. It was then that I realized how these photographs could form the ideal core around which to relate my tales, and *The Visitors' Book* is the result.

Mouzelle — Papa's governess and our unofficial family historian.

The Sykes Family

Introducing the principal characters in this Book: Great-great Grandpapa Tatton, 4th Baronet, founder of the Sledmere Stud, famed as rider & sportsman, stern parent of two sons & six daughters.

His son, Great Grandpapa Tatton, noted eccentric & traveller, who restored 18 wold churches & said he 'rued the day' he married...

The Dancing Marquis Grandmama Lily's first husband

...his young wife Jessica, generous & extrovert, whose tastes did not coincide & who consoled her boredom in various ways...

Her disapproving sister, Great-great Aunt Venetia, remembered for her thrift & snobbery

Tatton's younger brother Christopher who sacrificed his dignity, his fortune & finally his life to royalty

The Sykes Family

Grand-papa Mark, only child of Tatton & Jessica, cartoonist, cartographer & orientalist, man of letters & politics, founder of the Wagoner's Reserve, Lieut. Colonel of the Territorial Battalion the 5th Yorkshire Regiment, devoted husband & father of six.

Richard, the eldest son succeeded Mark at the age of 13,

he showed early promise as a film director & script writer & showman of the Sledmere

Cellars during the 20s & early 30s before he saw wartime service with the Green Howards.

Chapter 1
Great Great Grandpapa

IT WAS ONCE SAID of Great Great Grandpapa that, together with York Minster and Fountains Abbey, he was one of the three great sights of Yorkshire. The reason for this was that by the middle of the nineteenth century most grand country gentlemen had long since ceased to live in the manner of the great eighteenth-century squires, preferring to adopt the new ideals of Victorian society. In no way, however, did this apply to Sir Tatton Sykes of Sledmere who continued wholeheartedly to rule over a squirearchy in true eighteenth-century tradition. He was immediately marked apart from other men by his clothes. Right up to his death, in the age of pegtop trousers, he dressed each day in the old-fashioned manner of mahogany-topped boots, drab breeches, and a long-skirted, high-collared frock coat with a white neckcloth and frilled shirt. Then there was his Grandisonian style of speech, in which almost every sentence was rounded off with the word 'sir', although, when speaking with his tenants, he would adopt the native Yorkshire dialect. In either case, he spoke with a slightly high-pitched nasal voice.

Though his dress and mode of speech made him celebrated as an eccentric, it was for his reputation as a sportsman and a farmer that he was respected throughout England. His feats of endurance were legendary even in an age when country gentlemen prided themselves on their stamina and staying power, and were ready to match themselves to walk or ride tremendous distances, either against competitors or

When first Sir Tatton saw the light,
Our farms were in a wretched plight –
East Yorkshire Wolds were barren lands,
No better than the shifting sands
Of desert wild and wilderness,
Compared with what the scene now is.
Those vast uncultivated wilds
Are turned to rich productive fields.
This change was brought by him we call
Fourth baronet of Sledmere Hall.

He loved his horses, hounds, the chase,
And sometimes rode and won the race.
Unsparing his munificence,
Fine schools and churches rose from hence:
The house of Sykes with liberal hand,
Dispensed their bounty thro' the land,
And he whose death men now deplore,
Was helper to the helpless poor.
All classes do his loss regret:
Sir Tatton Sykes, fourth baronet.

From 'The Late Sir Tatton Sykes', George Whiting 1865

Great Great Grandpapa, whose eighteenth-century mode of dress immediately marked him apart from other men.

A groom holding one of Great Great Grandpapa's 320 horses.

against time. He had an aversion to coaches and railways and kept a string of horses all over the country, thereby enabling him to undertake long journeys, usually to attend race meetings. He would set off with his racing jacket under his waistcoat and a clean shirt and razor in his pocket. On one famous occasion he rode all the way from Sledmere to Aberdeen for the sake of a mount on a horse he particularly admired, returning via Doncaster in time to see the St Leger: a journey of 720 miles accomplished in eleven days. Even at the age of eighty, and in mid-winter, he still rode to London to sit for a portrait by Sir Francis Grant. Accompanied by his servant Tom Grayson, he rode about forty miles a day, making five halts, the first being at Selby. They started early each morning and proceeded at a sort of jogtrot all day, for, as Sir Tatton said of his horses, 'Give 'em time, and they can go on for ever.'

He was also an extremely accomplished pugilist, having taken lessons as a young man from two of the most famous fighters of the day, Gentleman Jackson and Jem Belcher. With his tall, wiry, muscular frame he had proved himself a formidable pupil. His father once journeyed to London to see a great fight, and on reaching the appointed place found to his horror that his son was one of the combatants. He returned home at once. Many are the tales told of Sir Tatton's pugilistic encounters, and this contemporary account of a meeting with some drovers is typical of them:

Sir Tatton Sykes the elder has a rather weak, squeaky voice. On one occasion he went into an inn for a glass of ale. There were a number of men in there sitting drinking. He asked for the ale in this rather thin voice and one of the men began to make fun of him. This raised the Squire's wrath. 'I'll fight you all round,' he said, 'one at a time. The loser will pay for drinks all round.' The offer was acclaimed with joy, for the men thought they would get their free drinks with very little trouble. They did not know that Sir Tatton was such a boxer and he gave the lot of them such a thrashing that they heartily wished they had been more polite to him.

So formidable did his reputation become that the question 'How's Sir Tatton looking?' was one of the first to be asked as each York and Doncaster meeting came round. Strangers sometimes descended from the grandstand as soon as he had been pointed out to them at his wonted place by the rails, and made a series of mysterious gyrations around him, in order to do full justice to the assurance that 'You'll never see such a man again.'

'T'aud Squire', as Great Great Grandpapa was affectionately known in Yorkshire, began his life as a younger son, his brother Mark Masterman having succeeded to the baronetcy on the death of their father Sir Christopher in 1801. Mark was also a keen sportsman, but combined his love of the chase with more aesthetic interests, as one of the most liberal patrons of the arts and literature of his day. His collection of the finest examples of early printed books made Sledmere as famous for its library as it was later to become for its bloodstock. Dibdin, in his *Bibliomania*, speaks in raptures of the '*editiones principes*, tall copies, rare specimens and uniques'. These included an early copy of Livy printed on vellum, and the two volumes of the Gütenberg Bible alongside which in the library catalogue are written the words 'I have never seen a finer example than this'. How Mark Masterman must have turned in his grave at the fate that befell his precious collection on his death in 1823, for Great Great Grandpapa had little time to spare for books, especially since one of his favourite packs of hounds was in desperate need of financial assistance. Consequently he held a three-day sale of the contents of the library at which he disposed of the cream of the collection, raising over £10,000 for his hounds from the sale of his books and another £24,000 from the sale of prints and portraits. His total lack of interest in the proceedings is reflected in his diary, the entry for those days containing no reference to the sale, only an account of the day's hunting.

The library, in which Great Great Grandpapa used to take his early morning exercises.

Though Great Great Grandpapa was fifty when he inherited Sledmere and its vast estates, he was still a bachelor, which immediately raised the problem of finding a son and heir. Being far too set in his ways, he had little taste for marriage himself and, as his younger brother Christopher only had daughters, this left the entailing of Sledmere on the male issue of his two sisters. One of these ladies, Decima Helen Beatrix Foulis, had a son called Mark whom Tatton duly tried to persuade to marry, suggesting as a suitable bride the young man's cousin Miss Mary Foulis. When Mark refused to comply with his uncle's wishes Great Great Grandpapa was finally driven to say, 'Well, if that is the case then there is nothing for it but for me to wed', and he rode off at once and proposed to Miss Foulis. It is unlikely that the lady could have been anything but flattered at such a distinguished offer of marriage, but she could certainly never have guessed what was in store for her.

The life to which Mary Foulis was introduced at Sledmere was a spartan one. The house itself, with its hall hung with agricultural implements and its huge rooms, was situated high up on the Yorkshire Wolds, and in those days, before the trees planted around it by Sir Tatton's father Christopher had matured, was still very much exposed to the chill north-eastern winds. As for her new husband, he lived according to a strict daily routine which he had no intention of changing for a woman. He would rise at half-past five, in both winter and summer, shave himself in cold water and wash his head. He would then put on his dressing-gown, slippers and breeches and go into the library. This great room, which overlooks the park, is over a hundred feet in length and he would walk up and down it, calculating the distance he covered by placing a piece of silver from the pocketful he carried on a table at the end of the room each time he completed the return journey. In this way he would often cover three or four miles before his breakfast, a meal that usually consisted of a basin of new milk and an apple or gooseberry tart, accompanied by lumps of mutton fat, and occasionally supplemented by a glass of stout and cream.

In the choice of food the new Lady Sykes again had little influence over her husband. He knew what he liked and preferred to stick to it. Once, when she and her family were going to London, she instructed the housekeeper to ask Sir Tatton every morning what he would have for lunch. That first morning he said 'Same as I had yesterday' and so, after finding out what Sir Tatton had eaten, she sent up the same dish. The next morning the reply to the query was identical: 'Same as I had yesterday.' This went on for nine days and the favoured dish was broad beans, bacon and new potatoes.

If this diet did nothing else for Great Great Grandpapa, it certainly kept him fertile. Great Great Grandmama bore her husband eight children – two sons and six daughters – and in their upbringing they were spared no hardships by their father who believed that they should be raised according to exactly the same standards by which he lived. They too were made to rise at dawn in both winter and summer, take cold baths, live in extremely spartan conditions (all six girls slept in one small room) and submit to frequent applications of the paternal whip. According to my uncle, Christopher Sykes, in his book *Four Studies of Loyalty*, 'When the sons returned from the squalor of school they were often greeted with flagellations which must have made them sigh for the birches of Harrow. On one occasion discipline was administered because, on unpacking, the unmanly frippery of toothbrushes was discovered among their effects. The elder boy, being the weaker of the two, was treated with special concern; the heroic old father was once seen armed with a whip driving the child barefoot and screaming down the drive.' This somewhat cruel behaviour is yet another example of how Sir Tatton was completely rooted in the eighteenth century, an age when parental oppression was considered quite normal.

Great Great Grandmama, Mary Foulis, whom Great Great Grandpapa married at the age of fifty.
She bore him eight children and resigned herself to his hard ways.

I do not think that Great Great Grandmama could ever accustom herself to her husband's treatment of the family, preferring however to resign herself to it rather than fight it. Consequently, while at Sledmere, she directed her attentions to the pleasures of gardening, in the magnificent orangery which stood in the grounds and among the numerous hothouses. More and more, however, she began to spend her time in London at the huge family house in St James's Place, overlooking Green Park, where she became a very fashionable hostess. The glittering social circle over which she presided included among its ranks such distinguished guests as the Duke of Wellington, then at the height of his popularity. Here she really was queen and on occasions when the old Yorkshire squire, fresh off his mount from Sledmere and complete with boots and spurs, burst into the middle of one of her entertainments, he would meekly allow himself to be stowed away, recognizing his limitations amongst fashionable London society.

Great Great Grandpapa greatly preferred to remain at Sledmere where he felt far more at home amongst the society of huntsmen and farmers, for whom the name of Sledmere became synonymous with endless hospitality and lashings of home-brewed 'Old October' ale. He had an ability to treat all men as his equals, to make friends of servants, of farmers and cattle drovers, stone-breakers and quaint rural or sporting characters, without in any way sacrificing his dignity. It was his firm belief that all work which was honest was also honourable, and he was certainly not averse to showing the workmen on the estate and farm that he would never expect them to do what he himself could not. He was fond of road-mending and would often take up a hammer to help a stone-breaker at his work, or take a turn with the turnip-hoers if there was nothing special going on in the paddocks that morning. It was quite common for him to be mistaken for a drover, as it was often his habit to drive his own stock along the roads, either from or to markets or to fresh pastures; once he even drove a flock of Bakewell sheep all the way from Lincoln to Sledmere, a journey of three days on foot. From time to time and for his own amusement he would adopt a disguise. One day he disguised himself and, accosting a drover who was driving some beasts along the road towards Sledmere, asked him where he was taking them. On being told they were

One of the reasons why Great Great Grandpapa was so popular was that he mixed freely in the company of farmers, cattle drovers and horse drovers, of whom the two pictured here would have been typical.
(overleaf) Great Great Grandpapa with Snarry the groom, holding the famous stallion Fandango, and Sir George Strickland.

for Sir Tatton, the baronet promised the drover he would 'help him up' if he would give him half of what he got, and to this the drover agreed. Sir Tatton quickly went home and told his bailiff to give the drover a sovereign. He then slipped out and, overtaking the drover, enquired how he had fared. He received the answer that he had only got a shilling for his work. Of course he never employed that drover again.

Great Great Grandpapa, incapable of doing anything in half measures, wished his reputation as a breeder of bloodstock to be as formidable as it was in other areas, and so built up his stud on a vast and unmanageable scale. The result was that quantity exceeded quality. In 1860, before the dispersal of his mammoth stud, he had no less than forty-six mares by Sleight of Hand entered in the Stud Book, hardly one of which had the honour of a name. They must have been about as distinguishable from one another as his sheep. Confirming this, a frequent visitor to Sledmere, Henry Hall Dixon, 'the Druid', wrote:

There were too many of them and hence no stud lived so hard out of doors. When grass was very scarce they had hay, varied at time with oats and chopped straw. Instead of reducing, Sir Tatton kept increasing his stock of brood mares and, unaccountable as it may seem, while he had some 320 head of horse stock, including hacks, he would never keep a pair of carriage horses, but hired post horses from Malton, and latterly the Sledmere Inn.

Along with all the second-rate animals, however, there were some very fine winners bred by Great Great Grandpapa, including St Giles, a winner of the Derby, and Grey Momus, winner of the Two Thousand Guineas and the Ascot Gold Cup, as well as Elcho, The Lawyer, Gaspard and Lecturer, to name but a few. He also bought the great stallion Fandango, winner of numerous races including the Ascot Gold Cup and the Great Metropolitan at Epsom in 1855, bidding 3,000 guineas for him at the Doncaster

sales. So anxious was he to buy the horse that, having made the bid, he immediately out-bidded himself by another 100 guineas. When he was reminded by Mr Richard Tattersall that he had made the previous bid as well, he merely pulled out his watch and said 'Knock him down, Mr Tattersall. Knock him down. We want to go to the races.' The foundations of the stud thus having been laid, it was to be left to Great Grandpapa to raise it to its greatest heights.

Before Great Great Grandpapa died in 1863 he completed one task which was to have far-reaching consequences, and that was the finishing of the work started by his father Sir Christopher, 'the Reformer of the Wolds', in whose time they were one vast, open field, destitute of hedges and ditches, with stones here and there to mark where one property ended and another began. Rabbits abounded and indeed some of the farms were considered good only for raising rabbits. The transformation of this barren wasteland had been Sir Christopher's lifelong work, and it was continued and improved upon by Great Great Grandpapa who himself made one of the most important discoveries in modern agriculture: bone manure. He had invariably kept a number of foxhounds at Sledmere, and always noticed the richness and profusion of grass around the area where they gnawed their bones. Intrigued by this, he decided to use bones as an experimental dressing, at first broken up as much as possible with hammers, and later crushed in a machine of his own invention. This initial test confirmed his suspicions and, though there were many people who laughed at him at the outset of his latest whim, he continued to use broken bones with such success that others speedily followed his example.

At the entrance to Sledmere Sir Tatton erected a well in the Grecian style as a memorial to his father. It bears an inscription which reads, 'This edifice was erected by Sir Tatton Sykes, Baronet, to the memory of his father Sir Christopher Sykes, Baronet, who by assiduity and perseverance in building, planting and enclosing on the Yorkshire Wolds, in the short space of thirty years set such an example to other owners of land, as has caused what was once a blank and barren tract of country to become now one of the most productive and best cultivated districts in the county of York.'

The gothic monument which the people of the Wolds built as a memorial to Great Great Grandpapa.
(opposite) Great Great Grandpapa erected this well in memory of his father's contribution to agriculture.

Great Great Grandpapa never achieved his secret wish to reach the age of a hundred. In November 1862, a year after the death of his wife, he suffered an attack of bronchitis which shook him still more and was aggravated by his dislike of doctoring and his forgetfulness of age. When the winter came he rarely went near his beloved paddocks to see the mares and foals, which those around him felt to be the strongest involuntary confession of increasing weakness. Early in March he had an attack of gout, which rather amused him than otherwise, seeing that his family had been subject to it and yet here was he, the premier sportsman of all England, only caught by it at ninety and a half. When it quitted him eight days before his death, dropsy rapidly set in, and the sad whisper 'Sir Tatton is dying,' although scarcely believed at first, spread through Yorkshire. He lay almost insensible but breathing very heavily from Tuesday to Saturday, and then his brave heart went out with the dawn.

Two years later the people of the Wolds demonstrated the reverence 'akin to idolatry' which they felt for Sir Tatton, with the building of a great Gothic monument on the summit of Garton Hill above Sledmere. An inscription on parchment was placed in a sealed bottle and deposited in a cavity in the foundation stone. Part of the text reads, ' "The memory of the just is blessed." A memorial, of which this is the foundation stone, was erected to the memory of the late Sir Tatton Sykes, 4th Baronet, by his tenantry and numerous friends, in testimony of his worth and the esteem in which he was held by all who had the privilege of knowing his many virtues in all the relations of life. To his tenants he was a liberal landlord and to the poor a kind and considerate friend.' Perhaps the most appropriate epitaph was that of his groom Snarry, who said, when the news of his master's death reached him, 'Aye, whya, there may be manny mair Sir Tatton Sykeses, the more the better, but ther'll nivver be another Sir Tatton.'

A MONODY

ON THE DEATH OF THE LATE SIR TATTON SYKES, BART.,
OF SLEDMERE.

One of Earth's nobles sleeps the sleep of Death,
And weeping friends consign him to the earth;
There to repose amid the silent dead,
Till Time, and all its changing scenes are fled.

Oh! for the painter's power, that I might trace
The holy calm that cloth'd that dying face!
Like a true hero on life's battle plain,
Brave to the last—unconscious of his pain;
Peaceful as infant on its mother's breast,
He gently sank to his eternal rest.

So should the good man die, whose glorious aim,
Was to uphold the honours of his name;
Whose high ambition changeless to the end,
Was to be called the Farmer's truest friend.

Rich beyond measure in all earthly goods,—
The fruitful valleys, and the waving woods;
Those were his own, far as the eye could scan,—
A noble heritage for such a man!
Years may depart, and we may hope in vain,
To look upon so true a man again. —
A better landlord never filled a grave—
One of Old England's bravest of the brave.

Vain the Historian's power, the Poets pen,
To sketch the lives of such like glorious men;
Above the surging tide of human life,
They stand like Heroes battling in the strife.—
Champions of freedom, faithful to their cause,
England's best bulwarks of her noble laws!
Well may we weep to see that aged head,
With silv'ry hairs laid lowly with the dead;
We ill can spare such men from Britain's isle—
Such lib'ral owners of her fruitful soil.

Peace to the dead!—he dies a good old age,
And leaves inscribed on history's hallow'd page
A name which will not from our mem'ry part,
But live endeared to every British heart.

Whatever faults he had, we name them not;—
In the true life he liv'd, they're all forgot;
We but remember, as through life we pass,
How good, how great, how generous he was.—
Peace to the dead! Your heart-felt grief restrain,
Good men and true, are sure to meet again.

Great Driffield,
  March 24th, 1863.   **J. TATE.**

Chapter 2
Great Grandpapa Tatton and Jessica

REAT GRANDPAPA TATTON was far away on an Eastern tour when the news of his father's death was brought to him. On hearing it the only words he could manage to utter were, 'Oh indeed, oh indeed, oh indeed.' This apparently cold, indifferent attitude becomes less surprising when it is remembered that he was that older boy against whom his father's wrath had so often been directed. The old man had had no room in his heart for a son who was weak and sickly and unable to compete with him on his own ground and who, in his opinion, was 'good for nowt'. The mother whom his son adored seems also to have had little time for him, preferring to lavish her attentions when at Sledmere on her garden and orangery, while the rest of the time she was away in London enjoying her social life. Great Grandpapa therefore grew up in an atmosphere devoid of love which moulded him into the strange, eccentric man he eventually became.

As soon as he was old enough, Great Grandpapa spent more and more time away from the life that had become so intolerable to him at Sledmere, making extensive tours abroad each winter and spring. These trips were perhaps among the happiest times of his life. A painfully shy man, he loved to travel alone and in this way he acquired a taste for solitude that was never to diminish. Travel also gave him the opportunity to indulge his passion for architecture, and he would often journey great distances to see famous cathedrals and churches. He rarely followed the beaten tourist track on his journeys, preferring to strike out on a line of his own, and few things worth observing escaped his notice. He paid several visits to Palestine and India; once he went to Japan, and amongst the many other countries he saw were China, Russia, Mexico and America, so making him by the age of thirty-seven, when his father died, one of the most travelled men of his generation. Would that he had written detailed and interesting diaries of these journeys, but there is nothing apart from one very dull account of a trip to Italy. Instead he would return laden with large boxes of magic lantern slides showing views of the places he had visited, with which, one supposes, he used to entertain his sisters during the long evenings at Sledmere.

Great Grandpapa in 1856, aged 30.

Great Grandpapa often returned from his travels bringing magic lantern slides with which to entertain the family at Sledmere. One of these shows a party exploring the frozen Niagara Falls, the other the type of steamer he might have travelled on moored in the Gieranger Fjord in Norway.

As soon as the news of his father's death reached him Great Grandpapa returned to Sledmere where he set about making some sweeping changes. The first of these was the three-day sale in September 1863 of the entire stud, an event that caused a sensation in the sporting world, and which was described in the newspapers as 'the most remarkable sale of bloodstock which ever took place in this or any other country!' Special trains were laid on from points all over the country to the local station at Fimber, and for several days before there were numerous arrivals in York and at Malton. Prominent amongst the visitors were distinguished foreigners from Austria, Spain, Russia, Prussia, France, Italy and the German states, with the British colonies well supported and breeders, buyers, trainers and commissioners from almost every district in the United Kingdom. One aspect of the new regime was immediately noticed and mourned by the reporter: 'Alas! for the old Sledmere hospitality, there was not a chop or crust to be had unless you paid for it.'

The object of the sale was to make a clean sweep so as to be able to start afresh with an eye for quality rather than quantity. With this in mind Great Grandpapa chose to retain one two-year-old chestnut filly from which to breed for his new stud. Her name was Wensleydale and, at the end of the three days, she was all that remained out of 110 lots of 'Oad Tats'' stud.

The next area upon which Great Grandpapa settled his attentions was the Sledmere gardens, which he set about destroying with a deliberation that may well have been motivated by the resentment he felt against his mother for having lavished more affection on them than ever she had upon him. The magnificent orangery was demolished; the hothouses were dismantled; not even the lawns were left intact for, giving the excuse that the grass needed 'turning' to make it grow better, he had them all ploughed up right to the very walls of the house. Throughout the village the cultivation of flowers became strictly forbidden. He considered them, he once said, to be 'nasty, untidy things' while, to a friend who remarked how much nicer some of the shrub gardens would look with patches of flowers in front of them, he replied 'No! No! No! I like to see the ground raked over, raked over, raked over,' repeating the words again and again as was his habit. From time to time he would make tours of inspection round the village, his walking stick at the ready to slash off the heads of any flowers he might come across. To the distressed villager who had emerged in time to witness a cloud of flying petals, he would declare, 'If you wish to grow flowers, grow cauliflowers!' On one of these occasions a tenant who refused to be converted from roses to vegetables spoke his mind plainly: 'Whya, it's this way, Sir Tatton. If you take t'flooers, you'll 'a'e ti tak my auld woman ez weel.'

Another of his peculiarities was a dislike of cottagers on the estate using their front doors and, in order to prevent them doing so, he insisted that the existing doors should be locked, barred and bolted at all times, some cottages even being built with false front doors. Some said this was due to his hatred of seeing women gossiping and, as he thought it a habit impossible to prevent, he would compel them not to gossip on their doorsteps. Others said that it was because of his dislike of seeing children running about in the village street, and that he wished to restrict them to playing in their back yards, a theory that is borne out by one contemporary who wrote, 'On one of my visits, some building was going on, I think it was the school. As children will, they loved to play about amongst the bricks et cetera. Sir Tatton said to the foreman, "Now if these children come bothering around I'll turn all their parents out of their cottages."'

Yet there were odd contradictions in his character for, at the same time as this occasional sternness and severity, he was capable of great kindness towards those in need. He had, for example, one workman who suffered from some illness requiring him to undergo periodical operations, and he always sent this man to one of the best London doctors, and arranged everything possible for his comfort and welfare. It is probable that this interest in the health of others was attributable to his obsession with his own health. As far as this was concerned Great Grandpapa was a hopeless hypochondriac, a state of mind that had developed since early days. In February 1855 his brother Christopher wrote scornfully in his diary of a conversation he had had with Tatton on the subject of a proposed trip to America: 'Tatton's been asking my advice about the old, old American story. "You see I have such a very delicate stomach, that is the thing." Should he journey between Dublin and Liverpool till he gets accustomed to it?' In later years Great Grandpapa used to say that his respectful treatment of his stomach was one of the things to which he attributed his long life. Respecting his stomach meant consuming quantities of milk pudding each day. Even when he went away, in order to avoid the slightest possibility of visiting any place where he could not obtain his daily ration, he would take his own cook with him whose sole responsibility was the preparation of these puddings. One wonders in how many grand hotels the poor lady must have prepared her homely dishes surrounded by mocking French chefs!

In addition to this constant worrying over his stomach he was also consumed by the belief that in order to remain in the best possible health at all times a person must attempt to keep his body at a constant temperature. The temperature he favoured, having spent so much of his life in that part of the world, was an oriental one and this is how he achieved it: 'On two chairs outside his special den', wrote a friend, 'were arranged different coats. On one there were heavy overcoats. They were all different colours and

Great Grandpapa, shortly before his marriage.
(overleaf) The hay harvest being gathered right up to the very steps of the house.

Jessica's parents, George Augustus Frederick Cavendish-Bentinck and Prudence Penelope Leslie, otherwise known as Britannia.
(opposite) Jessica, whose wilful nature is evident even in this early photograph of her as a child.

each was a perfect fit, made to go one over the other and allowing for size. He sometimes wore six coats. I have seen him in church gradually strip off four covert coats and ulster, and he still had a coat on.' His custom was to start the day wearing several overcoats which he would cast off as he got warmer. If out for a walk by himself at Sledmere he would never bother to pick up what he had taken off, the children of the village knowing that they would receive one shilling from his butler for every coat that they returned. Once, when he made a rare visit to Ascot races, his brother Christopher was mortally embarrassed when the Prince of Wales turned to him and, pointing at Great Grandpapa, said 'Who is that extraordinary-looking fellow over there? Why on earth do they allow people in the enclosure dressed in such ridiculous clothes?' Sometimes, as well as all the coats, Great Grandpapa would wear two pairs of trousers, and when he once got too hot sitting in a train he simply removed his shoes and socks and stuck his feet out of the window! His obsessions about his health, his hatred of flowers, his abrupt manner and his reclusive nature all earned him the reputation of a helpless eccentric. It is not surprising, therefore, that people were astonished when in 1874 they read of his engagement to be married, to a woman thirty years younger than himself.

Christina Anne Jessica Cavendish-Bentinck was the daughter of a prominent Tory MP, George Augustus Frederick, and a great grand-daughter of the fourth Duke of Portland. Her mother, the former Prudence Penelope Leslie, whose nickname Britannia was well suited to her overbearing personality, had a strict code of behaviour which she expected her daughters to live up to. The role of a daughter was to

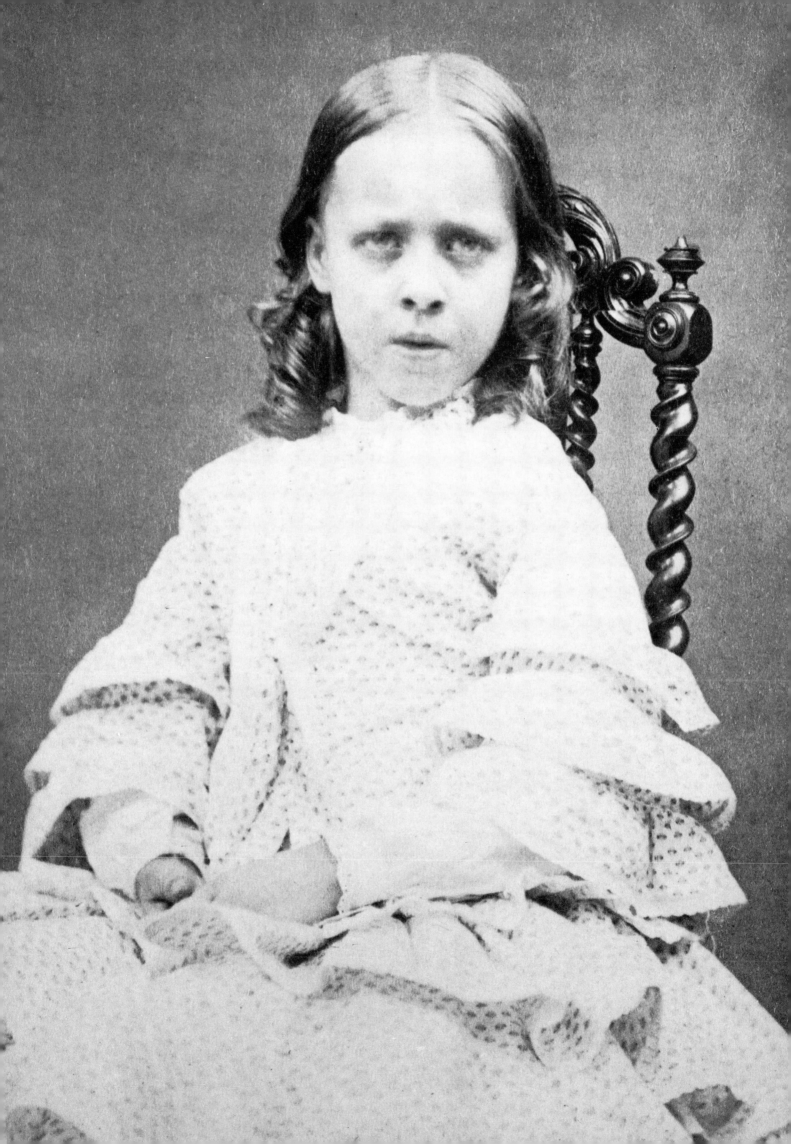

obey – first her mother, then her husband. Sons could do as they pleased. No matter the circumstances, Britannia believed that upper-class society must be protected at all costs, and to this end she expounded to her daughters the following code by which to live: that as long as women were pure, society would be safe; that men in exalted positions who possessed great wealth were subject to so many temptations that their behaviour was excusable; that no one should enquire too closely into people's private lives when they were members of the upper classes. While these rules were absorbed and adhered to by her younger and prettier sister Venetia, they cut no ice with Jessica. Striking in appearance, with a large square jaw and sharp, pale-blue eyes, she was far too intelligent and wilful to bend to such rules, and as a result she earned her mother's disapproval. With her father, on the other hand, she had much in common, for with him she could share her passion for horses and politics, subjects which were of far greater interest to her than those which a young lady was expected to enjoy. The Cavendish-Bentincks were a well-known sporting family and George Augustus Frederick would often take his daughter hunting or to the races, and she eagerly followed his parliamentary career. Under his wing, in his role as a politician interested in foreign affairs, she acquired a taste for travel, first attending art school in Paris, where she developed a talent for drawing and languages, and later accompanying the family on many journeys to Europe.

It was on one of these trips, to Bavaria in the summer of 1874, that there took place the fateful meeting with Great Grandpapa. Britannia, who made it her business to find out such things, knew that the gentleman whom the family had just met, Sir Tatton Sykes, was not only one of the richest men in England, with an estate of 36,000 acres and an income to match, but was at the same time a bachelor. Here it seemed was an ideal opportunity not only to make a great match, but also to get Jessica off her hands. However, she knew of Sir Tatton's reputation as a recluse and that it would therefore be up to her to ensnare him. With these factors in mind she formed her plan and put it into action without delay. She deliberately 'lost' Jessica for one night knowing that Sir Tatton would be the only person to whom her daughter could turn for help, and banking on the fact that he, as a gentleman, would be obliged to help her. When Jessica caught up with the rest of the party next day, escorted by Sir Tatton, Britannia feigned fury at her having been unchaperoned for a whole night. When they returned to England she went a step further by accusing Sir Tatton of compromising her daughter and he, to whom the idea of any kind of scandal was repulsive, proposed to Jessica. In her acceptance of this proposal, despite the enormous difference in their ages – she was eighteen while he was forty-eight – Jessica was motivated by two things. First of all, in those days, marriage was the only means by which a girl could get away from home, and Jessica longed to be free from her mother. Secondly she was, at the time, in love with another man, but when she told this gentleman about the proposal, instead of proposing to her himself, as she had hoped he would do, he replied, 'My dear Jessica, I think you would be well advised to accept Sir Tatton's offer.' That acceptance was to be the greatest mistake of her life.

Jessica and her sister Venetia. In later years, when Jessica was in trouble,
Venetia, then a fashionable socialite, refused to associate with her.

The wedding breakfast was as sumptuous an affair as the wedding itself.

The marriage of Great Grandpapa and Jessica took place in Westminster Abbey on 3 August 1874. It was a sumptuous affair. 'The wedding of the season', the Press called it, and its grandeur was well reflected by the glittering array of wedding gifts, from the bridegroom's 'suite of diamonds, consisting of a magnificent tiara, necklace of large brilliants, pendant, earrings, bracelet and set of eight brooches, forming head ornament, collaret etc., all of the finest water and most exquisite design, and a pearl necklace of four rows with fine diamond clasp', through those from the ranks of fashionable society right down to 'a gilt timepiece and aneroid barometer' from the servants at Sledmere, comprising altogether, in the words of the *News of the World* reporter, '325 gifts of a choice and costly description'. Britannia, 'richly dressed in pink silk trimmed with jet and Spanish lace' and undoubtedly ruling the proceedings, was escorted into the Abbey by the bridegroom to take her place triumphantly amongst the rows of aristocratic guests. It was, wrote one columnist, 'impossible for a masculine pen to do justice to such a scene of dazzling brilliancy'. After the wedding George Augustus Frederick gave a breakfast for 200 guests at his house in Grafton Street, and from there the bride and groom left to spend their honeymoon at Osterly Park as guests of the Duke and Duchess of Cleveland, before making their return to Sledmere.

Since Great Great Grandmama had died in 1861 the Sledmere to which Jessica was brought in the autumn of 1874 was much in need of a woman's presence, and the first months of her marriage were fully taken up with rearranging, redecorating and generally breathing life into the house once more. When she discovered to her horror that she had no flowers to brighten up the rooms, she imported huge palms and other potted plants which she placed strategically about the house, a fashionable compromise. She left her mark upon the library in particular, and the vast empty space where her father-in-law had taken his morning exercise was filled to overflowing with every conceivable sort of furniture, china, pictures, palms, screens, oriental rugs and bric-a-brac picked up on Great Grandpapa's travels.

Great Grandpapa and Jessica on their engagement.
(overleaf) The library as decorated by Jessica.

The house servants were a hierarchy in themselves.
At their head was the housekeeper, the formidable Mrs Tracy.

There was also, of course, the everyday running of a great house which for a girl of eighteen must have seemed a daunting task. To begin with, the staff alone numbered at least fifteen, and they were a hierarchy in themselves. At the head of them all was the housekeeper, the formidable Mrs Tracy, who ruled with a rod of iron over an army of housemaids. In the early hours of the morning they fluttered about the rooms like ghosts, dusting, polishing and laying fires. If possible they were never seen. In the pantry department the butler was master over an underbutler, two footmen or more, and a pantry boy. In the kitchen the cook was served by assorted scullery maids. Jessica, whose outgoing and extravagant nature was so different from that which everyone was used to in Sir Tatton, took it all in her stride and soon made herself very popular throughout Sledmere. With all the excitements of the new household the first few months of her marriage passed easily enough and it was not until things began to quieten down that the reality of the situation struck her: she had escaped from one prison only to find herself in another.

*The pantry staff, including two footmen complete with powdered wigs. (overleaf) This servants' group photograph includes
the butler, housekeeper, cook, an under-butler, one footman, and various maids.*

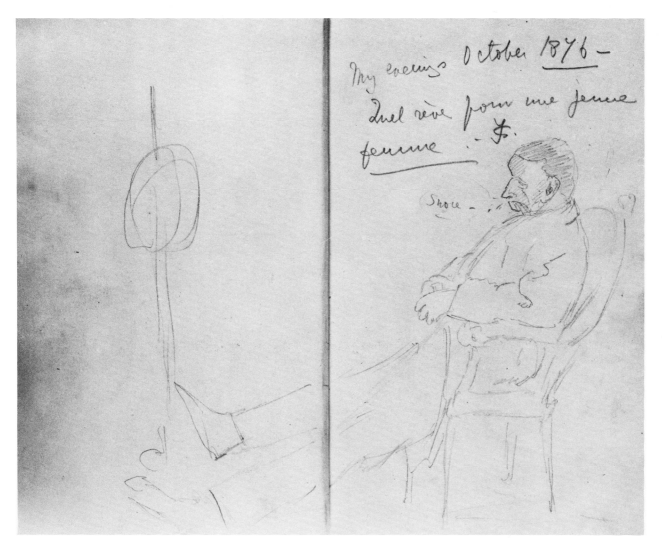

The pencil sketch of Great Grandpapa asleep which Jessica (opposite) made in the front of one of her hand-written novels.

It was not just the fact that she and Great Grandpapa were so different in age that made their marriage a disaster from the start, but that their characters were poles apart. While she was extremely extrovert, with a young girl's longing for gaiety and company, he, as we have seen, was deeply introverted and preferred to avoid the society of others as much as possible. His routine at Sledmere was, as his father's had been, a rigid one, and it was hardly designed to keep a young wife happy. He rose each day at six o'clock and, after taking a long walk in the park, ate a large breakfast before attending service in the church. He then retired to the estate office to deal with his business. Lunch at noon, with the inevitable milk pudding, was followed by a rest, more business, a light supper and then bed by eight o'clock. He did not smoke and the only alcohol that passed his lips was a wine glass of whisky diluted with a pint of Apollinaris water which he consumed each day after lunch.

Their incompatibility extended equally to the sexual side of the marriage, since Jessica's overtly sensual nature, which is so evident in her photographs, constantly clashed with her husband's natural shyness. In later years she was to confide to her daughter-in-law that it had taken six months for Tatton to consummate their marriage and, even then, only with the utmost clumsiness. 'Quelle rêve pour une jeune femme', wrote Jessica in 1876 under a drawing she had done of Great Grandpapa asleep in a chair.

Nevertheless, for the first few years of marriage Great Grandpapa and Jessica managed to live side by side in a reasonable manner. They had one thing in common at least, a love of travel, and together they visited not only the Continent but also Asia, Africa and North and South America, travelling in style and staying at the best hotels, and always accompanied by a cook to make the milk puddings. One feels, however, that even on these trips, when Great Grandpapa would have stuck to his routine, Jessica must have longed to sneak away, to make friends with fellow travellers and to go out at night. However she did score one point in her favour during this period by persuading Great Grandpapa to rent a flat in London, in Langham House, Portland Place, where she could entertain reasonably freely during the London season, knowing that he preferred to remain at Sledmere.

To pass the rest of the time she took up writing, and in her lifetime was to complete several novels, as well as some non-fictional works including a history of the Third Republic in France and a book on the Boer War. The novels were basically autobiographical. For example, in *Mark Alston*, she portrayed herself in the character of Portia Bulstrode, a rather ungainly and unmusical young woman, whose love of literature and art blossoms in Venice when she falls in love with Alston, a scholar engaged in a project on the scale of Plato's *Republic* and More's *Utopia*. This character was based on John Ruskin whom Jessica had befriended while staying in Venice. In the novel Portia saves every piece of paper he has touched, patterns her handwriting after his and falls completely under his spell. But Portia is forbidden to marry him by her mother who has already decided that she should marry Lord Beechfield, a forty-eight-year-old bachelor landowner. To her daughter's protests that she does not love Lord Beechfield Mrs Bulstrode replies that after her marriage Portia can do as she pleases.

If Great Grandpapa knew of Jessica's discontent then he chose to ignore it, as he considered he had far more important things to think about. The first of these was the realization of his one great romantic fantasy – the desire that, after his death, he should always be remembered as one of the corner-stones of the Gothic revival. Ever since his early travels, when he had been deeply impressed by the large number of people who made pilgrimages to the Holy Cities, and by all the crosses and memorials that had been built along the roads as a reminder of these journeys, he had longed to see a similar demonstration of the people's faith in the East Riding of Yorkshire. To this end, and with the help of a distinguished architect, Mr Temple More, he rebuilt and restored over fifteen churches in the East Riding, spending altogether the modern equivalent of over a million and a half pounds on the work. At the dedication of one of his restorations, that of the ancient church of St Hilda's, Sherburn-in-the-Forest, the Archbishop of York paid a tribute to him which he must have loved: 'There will always remain for him, among the wolds and plains of this part of Yorkshire, a memorial which time itself will not be able to efface – churches which by his love and reverence he has restored to the beauty which once adorned them in days gone by.'

If Jessica had had her own way there is one more great religious task he would have completed, and that was the financing and building of the new Catholic cathedral at Westminster, a project that obsessed her after her conversion to Catholicism. Her utter determination to persuade him to undertake this massive work made her certain she could bend his will, in spite of his serious misgivings about the cost. In January 1883 she wrote to Cardinal Manning, Archbishop of Westminster: 'Tatton has a dread the cathedral may eventually cost half a million, and wishes to work at it for two or three years before touching the capital – which is a little under £300,000. I will take care that, before he leaves England, a

Great Grandpapa rebuilt and restored over fifteen churches in the East Riding of Yorkshire,
including St Mary's, Sledmere, at the laying of whose foundation stone he is seen.
For Great Grandpapa these churches were a constant reminder of the faith of the people.

will is prepared and signed leaving this sum for the purpose he destined for it while it was accumulating.' It was lucky for the family fortune that Jessica's ambitions were never realized.

At the same time as Great Grandpapa was carrying on his Gothic crusade he was also concentrating on the rebuilding of the Sledmere stud, breeding from Wensleydale and from three other mares which he had bought himself – Miss Agnes, Little Agnes and Marigold. It was 'a strange contrast', wrote the Druid, 'to the old times when three or four stacks of eight or nine foals, haltered to each other so that they might learn to lead, were the object of a morning's walk.' As a brilliant judge of horses Great Grandpapa could now pick and choose each animal with great discrimination, and he was determined that, whatever total the stud might rise to, each mare had to possess enough individual character, quality and merit to raise her above the average. Thus when he was buying a mare the price was generally a secondary consideration. His methods brought spectacular success. As early as 1870 he had bred Doncaster,

A group of yearlings being led out in the morning.

destined to become one of the greatest horses in turf history, the winner of the Derby and second in the St Leger in 1873, later going on to win the Goodwood Cup and the Ascot Cup before becoming a successful stallion for the Duke of Westminster. Other notable horses he bred included Spearmint, winner of both the Derby and the Grand Prix de Paris, and sire of several Derby and St Leger winners; Mimi, winner of the 1000 guineas and the Oaks; Disraeli, first in the 2000 guineas and second in the Derby; as well as many, many more, all of whom contributed to making Sledmere a Mecca for the horse-racing world. Strangely enough Great Grandpapa never actually raced a horse himself. He bred only for the sales, and between 1890 and 1913 his progeny fetched for the stud close on £350,000.

In March 1879 Jessica gave birth to a son and heir whom she named Mark. It is clear that even at this early date the unsteadiness of her marriage was no longer secret, since rumours soon circulated that the child was in fact illegitimate, the son, some said, of a German baron, others, of the French actor Coquelin. Though there was ample evidence later on that the sexual inadequacy of her marriage drove her into the arms of many lovers, there was no basis for such rumours at this period, apart from what might or might not have happened on their travels abroad. However these rumours must have reached and unsettled Great Grandpapa for, when Mark was between three and four years old, he confessed doubts about the legitimacy of his son to a bank manager in York. This wise man, determined to set his client's mind at rest, told him that there was only one sure way to tell if a son was of his father's parentage, and that was if he walked in the same way as his father. He suggested that Great Grandpapa should take Mark out into the street and walk with him down towards the bank where he would be watching them from a first-floor window. If all was well he would wave a handkerchief. Father and son duly marched out into the street and, when they turned back, the bank manager, without bothering to make the comparison, waved his handkerchief. In his mind the very strong family resemblance was proof enough of legitimacy.

But Jessica was champing at the bit, and deep within herself she knew that she could not control her passions for much longer, the birth of a son having been only a temporary distraction. In desperation she turned to religion for strength, embracing the Roman Catholic faith into which both she and Mark were received in November 1882. But her inner struggle continued, as she wrote to Cardinal Manning on Christmas Eve 1882: 'Honestly, I am sorry for this – I have alas! no deep enthusiasm, no burning longing for perfection, no terrible fears of Hell – I am wanting in *all* the moral qualities and sensations which, I have been led to believe, were the first tokens and messages of God the Holy Spirit working in the human heart.' However, she declared herself willing to fight: 'Nevertheless I have a deep conviction of the entire truth of our Divine Lord's revelation through his church to mankind – a real reverence for goodness and wisdom and a desire to try and utterly abandon my sinful and useless life.'

The two sides of her existence became so opposed that it is difficult to understand how she managed to reconcile one with the other. Amongst the poor both in the East Riding of Yorkshire and in London she was celebrated for her extreme generosity and compassion. When she was in Yorkshire not a day went past without her dispensing food, clothes or money to some family in need, or pleading with her husband on behalf of some person in trouble. In Hull, where slum housing and general conditions for the poor were particularly bad, her work amongst poor children was famous, and Lady Sykes' Christmas Treat had become an important annual event. When she came down to London for the season she refused to allow her social life to interfere with her desire to help those less fortunate than herself, being shocked by the apparent indifference of most members of her class to the needs of the poor. She astonished people by her habit of going to balls until late at night and then rising early the next morning to do charity work with Father Brick from Farm Street, or to visit the girls' school she had established. Her kindness earned her a special name amongst the poor, 'Lady Bountiful'.

In London society people had another name for her: 'Lady Satin Tights', a name inspired by her increasingly wild behaviour. In order to gain greater independence from Great Grandpapa Jessica had leased a grand London house in the heart of Mayfair, 46 Grosvenor Street. Situated just off Grosvenor Square, with an imposing façade, grand staircase, and palatial rooms, this was the ideal house for entertaining, and here she behaved exactly as she pleased, smoking (a habit forbidden at Sledmere),

Great Grandpapa's only child Mark. At the time it was fashionable to dress little boys as girls.

(above and opposite) Jessica in two typically flamboyant poses.

drinking and gambling. With her keen mind and razor-sharp wit Jessica was excellent company and she attracted a wide circle of friends drawn from many different walks of life. There were members of the 'old guard' such as the Duchess of Montrose, who was a lively match for Jessica with her majestic manner and extraordinary command of pungent Johnsonian language, and the Duchess of Cleveland, who once said about some people of whom she disapproved, 'They are not nice people. They are not gentle people. Had they been poor they would have committed crimes.' There was the dashing Lord Charles Beresford who was something of a national hero after his participation in the bombardment of Alexandria, and the Nile expedition. There were politicians like Lord Randolph Churchill, a cosmopolitan sprinkling of ambassadors and diplomats with whom she had struck up acquaintance on her travels, as well as the inevitable literary figures such as Max Beerbohm; and of course no great society house was complete without visits from the Prince of Wales.

Lady Sykes' ball on Thursday night was a distinct social success, although HRH did not arrive till nearly one. The dancing was in the back drawing-room lit up with electric light. Mr Liddell furnished the music; 'Ce bon Christophe' did the honours (*vice* Sir Tatton), and Prince Henry of Orleans was amongst the guests. Supper was served in a tent hung with tapestry, and the hostess wore white with pink roses and a broad, pale-green sash. Mr Albert Stopford led the cotillon admirably; the Prince of Wales never danced with greater vigour. The cotillon did not end till after four and the sun was shining brightly when Lady Sykes' friends departed.

If the combination of society, good works and religion had been enough to fulfil Jessica then all would have been well, but her powerful nature demanded more from her. In 1890, while on a visit to Egypt with Great Grandpapa and Mark, she embarked on a passionate love affair with Jack Gorst, later to be Under-Secretary for Finance in Cairo and whose sister Edith was to become her daughter-in-law. It was those qualities in her that might have disturbed others among her contemporaries that drew him to her: her

57

frank direct manner, for example, and hatred of the double standards that were so prevalent in that period. 'If I have any vices,' she used to say, 'they are only those of a man.' She never talked down to anybody, believing that snobbery was stupid and silly and that people were only important for what they did, not who they were. 'She exercised', wrote Gorst in his diaries, 'a great influence over my life for the next two years and undoubtedly contributed very largely to the formation of my character and general views of life during that period. Some years older than myself, she possessed great intelligence coupled with an extraordinary variety of knowledge and a force of character unusual in one of her sex. All these qualities made her in those days a most delightful and instructive companion.'

Over the next two years Jessica and Jack spent as much time as possible together, both in Egypt and when he was on leave in England. Their lovemaking was recorded by Jack in his diary with a series of Xs and Os, totalling the score at the end of each year. For Jessica this affair brought the extremes of happiness she so needed when they were together, but unbearable anguish when they were apart which she tried to soothe by drinking more and more heavily. Her drinking, however, made her promiscuous, and so it was a vicious circle. Soon the times when they were together became too intense for Jack, and he felt himself compelled to end the affair, which he did in July 1892. 'Though the terrible failing which has been the cause of the termination of our friendship was supposed by popular rumour to exist long before our aquaintance began, I saw no signs of it in the first two years. It has only been very slowly and reluctantly that I have been forced to admit that, at all events latterly, popular rumour has been right. When once this conviction was brought home to my mind, I could not do otherwise than bring to a close a friendship which could be productive of nothing but sorrow.' Jessica never forgave Jack for the rather cold and short manner in which he ended their affair (the entry in his diary for that day read simply, 'Heard from J and decided that our liaison had better come to an end. Wrote acc'y') and it set her off on the path to self-destruction. It is both surprising and sad that even her great strength could not defeat the devil within her, for otherwise history might have remembered her more for her many admirable qualities than for her humiliating downfall, the circumstances of which were as follows.

By the mid 1890s Jessica's drinking had become so bad that her maid had resorted on several occasions to hiding her scent lest she take to drinking it again. Sometimes, when Jessica was in a particularly bad state, she took to hiding her stays so that she could not go out and disgrace herself while haunting the bookmakers' shops in Henrietta Street. Jessica had also taken to gambling heavily at the tables, and this compulsive behaviour made her even more desperate as she had to meet her losses in any way she could. Up until now she had always relied on Great Grandpapa to pay for her, but a change had taken place at Sledmere. Great Grandpapa's nephew Henry Cholmondeley, a hard-headed businessman, had taken over as his agent and discovered that Jessica had been drawing on the estate account. On his advice, and with his backing, Great Grandpapa now refused to give in to her pleas for more money, and the bills at 46 Grosvenor Street began to pile up. She made things still worse by resorting to money lenders with exorbitant interest rates and by speculating on the Stock Market. Even Mark was approached for loans from his allowance, or pleaded with to make representations on her behalf to his father. Her friends began to abandon her. But despite the many days during which she was drunken and pitiful, the old bravado remained. On hearing of her mother's death in 1896, for example, she shocked all around her with the remark, 'How like mother to die in Ascot week.'

In December 1896, on the advice of his solicitors who convinced him that it was the only way of

Jack Gorst, whose affair with Jessica lasted two years and the ending of which proved too much for her to bear.
He was later to become Consul-General in Egypt, from 1907 till 1911.

Henry Cholmondeley, a hard-headed businessman and a brilliant huntsman.

keeping Jessica's debts from spiralling further, Great Grandpapa took an unprecedented step. He took advantage of an amendment to the Married Woman's Property Act, whereby a husband could free himself of all debts subsequently incurred by his wife, by advertising to this effect in the newspapers – and he became the first man ever to publish such a notice. It appeared in *The Times* on 7 December:

I, Sir Tatton Sykes, Baronet of Sledmere in the county of York, and 46 Grosvenor Street in the county of London, hereby give notice that I will NOT BE RESPONSIBLE for any DEBTS or ENGAGEMENTS which my wife LADY JESSICA CHRISTINA SYKES may contract, whether purporting to be on my behalf or by my authority or otherwise.

Dated the 5th of December 1896

TATTON SYKES

The effect of this advertisement, repeated a week later in accordance with the law, was that all Jessica's creditors queued up for payment. Her usual solution of borrowing from one to pay off another no longer worked as no one would lend her any more money. She was finally forced to sign an agreement whereby, if Great Grandpapa paid her £12,000 'to discharge my present liabilities', and guaranteed her future receipts of £5,000 per year in addition to 'pin money' out of which she would pay 'all household and stable accounts in London', then she would 'promise not to speculate any more on the Stock Exchange or to bet for credit on the turf'. But although at the time this seemed to have settled things once and for all, there were still massive debts that Jessica had kept secret, and by the spring of 1897 the creditors were once again banging at the door. This time Great Grandpapa refused to budge. As a last resort Jessica decided to file a petition for divorce, but she soon dropped this when she realized, after the family lawyers had had an affidavit upheld stating that Great Grandpapa's net income was no more than £17,000 per annum, that she would not get as much alimony as she wanted. Things finally came to a head in January 1898 when a money lender, one Daniel Jay, brought a court action against Great Grandpapa and Jessica to recover the sum of £15,780 which was the amount of five promissory notes which he claimed had been signed by them both. Jessica admitted her liability and stated in her evidence that she had seen Great Grandpapa sign the notes, and that they were negotiated with his full knowledge and consent. Great Grandpapa, on the other hand, denied that he had signed the bills or that he had any knowledge of the transactions, and he further asserted that his 'signatures' were in fact forgeries.

The case naturally caused a sensation, and the courtroom was crowded out with people eager to hear the details of this extraordinary marriage. The spectacle was a sad one. There stood Jessica, proudly asserting Great Grandpapa's full co-operation in her borrowing, and attempting to discredit his testimony that he had no knowledge whatsoever of the affair by presenting him as a figure of ridicule, with absurd eccentricities and 'tiresome' meanness. Laughter filled the courtroom when she answered, in reply to a question as to Sir Tatton's abilities as a businessman, that he was 'as capable as most women'. When Great Grandpapa was called, he presented a rather pitiful sight as he shuffled into the witness box, weak from a bout of bronchial pneumonia and presumably weighed down by overcoats. He hated having to defend himself against accusations that he was a liar, and he hardly endeared himself to the court by dealing with it and the opposing counsel 'in a way which suggests he must be a very difficult person to deal with in private life'. Not even Mark escaped being forced into the witness box to testify as to which of his parents was telling the truth. So vague were his whispered replies to the questions of counsel for the plaintiff that Sir Edward Clarke, counsel for Great Grandpapa, waived cross-examination, saying the poor boy might have been spared the ordeal. When the time came for the final speeches Sir Edward did not waste any sympathy on Jessica, describing her as a woman of 'discreditable character', in whom there could be 'no credence'. For the plaintiff Mr Lawson Walton appealed to the jury to consider that 'the disaster of victory could be infinitely greater to Sir Tatton than the disaster of defeat . . . . At present Sir Tatton might wish to win the case, but in the evening of his days would he wish his name to be clouded with the dishonour of his wife?' The trial lasted three days at the end of which, after an absence of only thirty-five minutes, the jury returned the following verdict: the signature on the promissory notes and letters of authority were not in the handwriting of Sir Tatton Sykes. To complete Jessica's humiliation the Press went to town!

The glimpses of a millionaire's household which this trial has afforded us are anything but edifying. We fancy few people will waste much sympathy on either Sir Tatton or Lady Sykes. Of the latter it is best to say as little as possible. It is a shameful story on any estimate of the witnesses – the old story of May and December marrying for money. The spectacle of marriage in high life is worthy of Hogarth: and it is faintly hoped it may tend, as his pictures tended, to dissipate a little of the glamour with which these gilded creatures – gilded but of very common clay – are surrounded in the eyes of many simple folk. Revelation after revelation show that the tone of society is getting lower and lower, that religion, refinement, even rational and sober ideas of life are disappearing, that wealth and luxury are eating away the old aristocratic virtues. The law courts unroll one tale after another of meanness, emptiness and even crime among these people. We see no kind of purpose in such lives, save the pursuit of the emptiest kind of 'pleasure'. They run to the lowest financial trickster, the most unscrupulous and vulgar parvenu. And the most surprising thing is that within their own ranks no effective and dignified protest arises.

When the financial wranglings were finally over and the creditors all paid off, Great Grandpapa crept back to Yorkshire to hide himself away. Jessica gave up the house in Grosvenor Street and moved to 2 Chesterfield Street which had been left to her in the will of her brother-in-law Christopher. She tried hard to reform herself, giving up gambling and attempting to cut down on her drinking. She revived her interest in politics and journalism. When the Boer War broke out she saw an ideal opportunity to make herself useful, and so she set off for South Africa with two suitcases loaded with Bovril, jelly, tobacco and a box of Catholic prayer books provided by the Truth Society. Her destination was a convent in Natal which had been converted from a boarding school into a hospital for the treatment of typhoid. When she returned to England early in 1900 she took up writing again and published *Sidelights on the War in South Africa* in which she aimed some pertinent criticism at the rôle of the British government. It was, she wrote, 'the old story we have heard so often in India and other distant lands . . . of a government department in England attempting to govern a country which none of its members have even seen,' and she foresaw that the war would drag on much longer than people at home thought. She also made regular contributions to the *Review of the Week*, along with Bernard Shaw and others, and at the end of 1901 founded her own weekly, the *Sunrise*, which was a mishmash of political gossip and Roman Catholicism, 'the sort of journalism that makes me foam with rage', wrote Mark. She completed another book, *The New Reign of Terror in France*, which was a vitriolic attack on the Third Republic and the Dreyfusards, and she even tried her hand at playwriting. One of her plays was rejected by Herbert Beerbohm Tree on the grounds that its subject matter – a jockey's seduction of a lady – was too advanced for West End theatres. How like Jessica to dream up such a plot!

As for Great Grandpapa, who had hoped to be able to live out the rest of his days in peace at Sledmere, he was to be struck by yet another disaster.

Chapter 3
The Great Fire of Sledmere

N 23 MAY 1911 a fire broke out at Sledmere which led to the almost total destruction of the house, leaving only the four outer walls, the dairy and the laundry intact after a blaze which lasted almost eighteen hours. The fire started early in the morning when a beam which protruded into the kitchen chimney first began to smoulder, and then caught alight, the flames slowly spreading up into the roof where they really took hold. It was not, however, until about half past twelve that Henry Cholmondeley, noticing some suspicious-looking smoke coming out of a chimney, discovered on further investigation that the whole of the upper north-east wing was ablaze, and he sounded the alarm. Great Grandpapa, innocent of these events, was in the middle of his lunch, enjoying one of his favourite milk puddings, when Henry burst in to tell him that the house was on fire and that he must leave at once. 'First', said Great Grandpapa, 'I must finish my pudding, finish my pudding.'

When the great bell of the hall sounded the alarm all the men employed in the stables, the home farm and the wood yard were also at home for their lunch. As soon as they heard the news they rushed back up to the house where they were organized into a salvage corps. Messages had been despatched to the local fire brigades at Driffield and at Malton and, while their arrival was awaited, a chain bucket service was started which proved totally inadequate owing to the difficulty of reaching the heart of the fire. A supply of hose pipe brought by the Superintendant of the Malton Fire Brigade in his motor car and attached to one of the hydrants close to the house also proved useless as the pressure from the reservoir, which was normally only used for household purposes, was far too low and only small jets of water could be played on the blazing building. By now it was clear that there was little chance of saving the house from destruction without the assistance of the local brigades, of whom there was still no sign, and so all energies were concentrated on salvaging whatever possible from the contents of the house. A human chain, with the men at the head, then the women and even the village school children at the tail, stretched from deep within the house and spilled out on to the lawn. Along it were passed china, books, carpets, furniture, or whatever was remotely rescuable. 'The servants', commented the *Malton Messenger*, 'behaved with wonderful pluck and coolness in removing furniture from the burning rooms, the maidservants acting as coolly and bravely as the men!' Outside the library windows another group held out sheet and blankets into which were thrown the hundreds of books.

By the time the Driffield Fire Brigade arrived, soon after two o'clock, the fire, fanned by a slight breeze,

(overleaf) Great Grandpapa pacing up and down in his overcoats while, in front of him, Sledmere blazes.

*The combination of the slow progress of the fire and the help of the villagers
was responsible for the rescue of most of the contents of the house.*

When the flames had finally died down after burning for almost eighteen hours,
all that was left of the house, other than the laundry and the dairy, was a smouldering shell.

was rapidly gaining a hold. The manual engine was quite unequal to projecting water as far as the roof which soon caved in on the east wing. The Malton Fire Brigade finally trotted in at about three o'clock, having been delayed by difficulties with their horses and the steep hills they had had to climb. Immediately they put to work their powerful steam pumps which operated at great pressure and sent streams of water on to the roof and into the blazing upper stories. By now, however, it was too late and all that could be usefully done was to keep the walls of the rooms sufficiently cool while rescue operations were carried out. These were continuing in conditions which by now had become extremely dangerous, with the roof caving in piecemeal and burning debris raining down on the workers. Another hazard was the molten lead from the roof which poured down the walls until they alone were left standing, and splashed anyone who came too close. In spite of all this the men remained undeterred. As one huge picture was precariously carried down a burning staircase, the under-gamekeeper was heard to mutter, 'Now lads, don't damage t'frame.'

The scene on the lawn in front of the house was an extraordinary one with furniture and fittings, beautiful pieces of china, mahogany doors removed from their hinges, bed linen and mattresses, valuable paintings, treasure of silver and gold lying strewn around as they had been brought from the blazing building. Hundreds of books lay piled upon the grass as they had been thrown from upper windows, their pages fluttering in the wind. Amidst it all sat Great Grandpapa. 'To the eye of a connoisseur', wrote an eyewitness, 'it was a heart-rending sight, and to the owner, a solitary figure watching the tongues of

69

fire pursuing their destructive course, it must have caused many a pang of inward regret. Yet all he said when a word of sympathy was offered was, "These things will happen, these things will happen", repeating the words with resigned fortitude and recognizing the utter hopelessness of it all.'

He had one final wish, which was that an attempt should be made to save a beautiful marble copy of the Apollo Belvedere which stood in the entrance hall and which had been left till last as it was thought unlikely that the flames would reach it. Scores of hands volunteered to remove the statue. Jets of water were poured on the ceiling and the hall flooded. Water was also poured on the wall behind the statue, which was itself checked to render it cool enough to handle. The front door was removed and the jambs wrenched down to allow the passage of the life-size figure. With admirable skill it was lowered from its pedestal into the arms of the farm labourers and helpers and, with barely a break or a scratch, it was finally carried out to the lawn. The rescuers were only just in time for they had scarcely got outside when the ceiling fell in, and a column of sparks stood for an instant where the effigy had rested. This was the last incident of salvage possible.

Having seen his beloved statue rescued, Great Grandpapa could not bear to remain any longer and he left with Henry Cholmondeley to spend the night at the Station Hotel in York. There he was joined by Mark who had set off from London as soon as he had heard the news. When Mark arrived at Sledmere the following morning the scene that greeted him was a sad one, with the still-smoking, blackened ruins of the house providing a dramatic contrast to the rich, green foliage of the trees around them, and the stink of damp, charred wood mingling with the heavy scent of spring blossom in the air. On the lawn the valuable collection of china was roped in under the watchful eyes of special constables from Driffield, while the servants were busily engaged carting away furniture and pictures and placing them wherever suitable storage could be found in adjacent buildings. 'One of the most curious sights as one looked on to the roofless building', wrote an eyewitness, 'was a fire-place on the first floor, with paper, sticks and coals, which had never been touched by the flames that had lapped round and round it, blackening the walls and woodwork, but leaving it still ready for lighting.' Mark realized that, with the possible exception of the outer walls, the entire house would have to be rebuilt. When Great Grandpapa returned later in the afternoon it was agreed that this work would be carried out as soon as possible, using the original plans and copies of the decorative schemes which were still in their possession, to reproduce the house as faithfully as possible. Sadly it was a project Great Grandpapa was never to see realized.

In spite of being thirty years younger than her husband, Jessica failed to outlive Great Grandpapa. The drink saw to that for, however gallant her attempts to moderate it, they were always hopeless. She died in 1912 after a series of seizures, and was buried at Sledmere, her body having been brought up from London on a special train. At the memorial service held for her at Westminster Cathedral the chosen text was 'Charity covers a multitude of sins'. It was an appropriate epitaph. As he made his way out Great Grandpapa was heard to mutter, 'A remarkable woman, Jessica, a remarkable woman, but I rue the day, I rue the day I met her.'

Soon after his return to Sledmere he became convinced that at 11.30 one morning he too was going to die. Each morning his mount, an old cob, was brought round for him to ride. On some days he would go out, while on others he would send his groom away saying, 'No, no, can't ride, can't ride, going to die, going to die.' When he finally did die in May 1913 in London, it was at 3.00 a.m. after having suffered for three weeks from pneumonia. There was an eccentric note even to his death. He had been staying at the Hotel Metropole, and the manager begged Mark to allow the body to be removed from the premises hidden in a hollow sofa specially constructed for such occasions. Mark was outraged by the request. 'However my father leaves this hotel,' he cried, 'he shall leave it like a gentleman.' Eventually he agreed to a compromise, and Great Grandpapa's body was removed from the hotel in the secrecy of the night.

FUNERAL OF LADY SYKES

FUNERAL OF LADY SYKES.

On the day of her funeral Jessica's body was brought up from London to Sledmere on a special train.
The whole village turned out to bid her farewell.
(overleaf) Great Grandpapa's funeral procession, the following year, was preceded by forty schoolgirls, dressed in white
with black sashes, who lined the path to the grave and scattered posies of cowslips in front of the funeral party.

Chapter 4
Great Great Uncle Christopher:
'The Great Xtopher'

HE STORY OF Great Great Uncle Christopher is a somewhat tragic tale of a clever and sensitive man destroyed by a single weakness of character. He was a snob, with a passion for society which, as a young man, his better nature made him fight against and try to control, but which in the end was to take him over completely and lead to his downfall. This weakness stemmed directly from his upbringing. Like his elder brother Tatton, Christopher had grown up to fear and detest his father but, while the former sought escape in oriental travel and solitude, he chose the glitter of the London drawing-room, an area in which he knew his father to be exceedingly uncomfortable. His success as an up-and-coming young socialite failed to impress the old Squire, who was once heard to remark, 'Christopher's only good for handing ladies into their carriages.'

After leaving Cambridge in the early 1850s Christopher kept a series of extremely detailed journals which present us with with a vivid portrait of his life and character as a young man. They reveal his constant disillusionment with society and his deep-rooted guilt at leading what he considered to be an idle and useless life. On visits to Sledmere (whose never changing life-style he portrays beautifully) he was able to concentrate on his love of more intellectual pursuits, yet in the end he was always either drawn or driven back to London. In his journals he describes the frivolous and shallow atmosphere of the London season with a sharp and witty pen; the journals also reveal that he was desperately jealous of Tatton's position as the eldest son. They begin in 1852 when Christopher was twenty-one.

Sunday 2 May 1852: Hamilton Place

Dinner bad: no soup and fish which produced a loud groan from me when I perceived their absence. Beef high. Tatton said, 'Nobody could wish for a better dinner.' I, choking with rage, and high beef and hunger, denied it. Tatton, after dinner, gave us a red-hot Protestant lecture, apropos of St Barnabas. His arguments were those of an illiterate greengrocer.

Friday 18 June

Dined with Mr and Mrs Blackwood last night. The dinner vile, the company worse. Mrs Blackwood, the most vulgar woman I ever met. Sat by Miss Blackwood; rather pretty and nice. A deaf and dumb man on the other side of her. He made awful noises. My nerves, shaken with sitting up until three every morning

Great Great Uncle Christopher, a sensitive young man,
the two sides of whose nature were in constant conflict

for the last two months, almost gave way. I thought I should have got up involuntarily and run out of the room. Mr Blackwood exclaimed in the middle of dinner: 'You are a very ill-behaved fellow. You never answered my invitation.' The creature had put 'to remind' on it and evidently did not know that that required no answer. Mrs Blackwood said she did so like looking at her husband when asleep. Indelicate brute! Been reflecting whether I should like really to marry or not. Think decidedly not. Ate part of an iced pudding and could not make out if it was iced or not; a sort of dreadful cold heat about it. However I escaped at last and went with Adeane to Lady Isabella Stewart's.

Saturday 19 June

Went to Lady Salisbury's. Flew about the room endeavouring to get to the Duchess of Beaufort's on Monday, but without success. Took Lady Westminster to her carriage and had to wait an hour in the hall, and then to walk all down Piccadilly in the rain to look for it. Hope such devotion may be rewarded.

24 June

Dined at Lady Bradford's last night. Lady Westminster gave me half one finger to shake. Ingratitude after going all down Piccadilly for her carriage.

25 June

Went to Lady Glamis' ball in the evening. Lady Loudes pumped me as to Annesley's and my own expectations. I gave her to understand I was not a younger son according to the general acceptance of the term. Much pleased by Ramsden telling me that Lady Lucan said I was a concentrated lump of amiability.

1 July

Dined at Mrs Egerton's last night. Met Colonel and Mrs Murray, the author of the new work on Australia. It was curious to hear all the particulars of Australian life and to think of the scenes and hardships there people must have gone through, seated at the little round table in my aunt's boudoir, covered with plate and the most costly china, the groom of the chambers and his regiment around. It is so seldom in fashionable society that one meets anybody with two ideas in their heads.

8 July

Dined with Admiral and Mrs Ferguson last night. Quite a small party at a round table. The Admiral was dreadfully personal with his poor daughters. I quite felt sorry for them. It reminded me so of Sledmere. I took Ramsden on to Lady Aylesbury's. With my usual ill luck as I ascended the staircase I met Lady Aylesbury proceeding down with considerable circumstance followed by an old lady in a light brown wig. I stooped forward and said, 'Lady Lucan said your Ladyship was good enough to ask me.' She was very gracious but appeared surprised; the whole party moved on, the old lady nearly stumbling over my foot; another moment and I remembered it was the Duchess of Gloucester proceeding to her carriage and that I had stopped Lady Aylesbury in her sort of progress downstairs. Could anything be so unlucky. A crowd in the rooms. Lady Lucan civil. D . . . gave me a most insolent nod, leaning over Lady Lucan's chair. I hope he didn't tell her I was only the younger son.

10 July

Went to Lady Gage's. Lady Lucan asked me to take a walk with her in the garden. Down we went and she talked in a very distrait, odd way for some time, evidently not thinking of what she was saying. At last,

Lord Annesley, a social butterfly who took Christopher's friendship for granted.

with more energy than she had yet displayed, she said, 'Pray Mr Sykes, have you many brothers?' 'Oh, no!' I exclaimed, 'only one.' She then said, 'Oh, somebody said you had several. But your brother is older, is he not?' 'Yes,' I said, then began a story about being taken for the elder son, but she assured me that she had always said I was the younger one. 'Now,' she said, 'it is getting damp. We had better go in.' I was nearly assuring her I was not a younger son in the basest acceptation of the word. Walked home with Ramsden. Two horrid women seized me and almost carried me off. I am glad the London season is over.

13 July

So the end of the great London season has really come at last, and finds me I think just the same as when it began. I have seen nobody I admire, and I have made few new acquaintances. I have been about as unhappy and as discontented as usual all the time, and am now sorry to go away. Shall I marry next year or not?

Last day in London

After a hot afternoon spent in the city getting a Belgian passport, I put on my hat and sauntered into the park. Here, leaning solitary and languid over the rails, contemplating the 'swells' as they rode by, I encountered Annesley. 'Lord! how melancholy and *delabré* you look in that seedy old great coat,' was his Lordship's exclamation. I was dressed in a clean white waistcoat, patent leather boots, new trousers and a light-blue great coat. This was being *delabré*! He proceeded to tell me he had secured stalls at the Opera for two guineas each: this was too much for my feelings, fresh from examining my account book and its deficit. The worm almost turned, and I made him confess they were only a guinea. 'Do come,' said he, 'it is the last night I shall see you,' and, seeing me hesitate, added as an attraction 'and you can tell me your beastly plans.' Strong contemptuous emphasis used. He offered to take me in his brougham or I to take him. I foolishly acceded to the former. I went home. After a hurried dinner and before I could get my much-loved cup of tea, his Lordship's brougham was announced and in I bolted, and then waited to pick him up at the Coventry. 'Oh,' said he, 'my dear fellow, can you manage to get home alone, for Charlie Webster has promised to take me at eleven to see the new ballet.' With my usual pride I begged he would not think of me. 'What a coat! Is it a coat?', poking my new and fashionable opera cloak. On the road we talked about the blessings of riches. When we arrived at the Opera our stalls were immediately under the boxes of Lady Howard de Walden and Lady Carrington. His Lordship was frantic and restless until he left the stalls and rushed into the boxes where he sat in Lady Carrington's with Augustus Lumley, leaving me feeling very wretched and lonely, with a sort of horrid feeling that he and the Carringtons were looking at me which made me not know which way to look. At length I met him rushing about the lobby looking for Charlie Webster. 'Goodbye. I am looking for Webster, where is he? Take care of yourself. Is he gone? Write to me.' This was his adieu for a year or so. I was in dreadfully low spirits all the opera and could not enjoy it at all.

I wrote this long story about Annesley in order to remind myself next year not to become too dependent for society on a person so capricious and thoughtless as he, and who, though kind and excellent, certainly would not put himself out of the way for me.

Sunday 26 March 1854: Sledmere

Back from a long trip to Italy. When I come back here all the time I have been away seems like a dream. Everything is exactly the same here; the same conversation, the same jokes, the books in the same place on the same tables. My rooms just as I left them. One cannot believe that five months full of incident and excitement have passed away. Home seems very calm and comfortable; a refuge quite inaccessible to any of the vexations and fatigues of the world.

3 April

I am enjoying myself here exceedingly; the days are not long enough; the weather is lovely, bright sunshine: trees are all coming out, the air so sweet and fresh. From half past eight until a quarter to eleven I translate Lamartine's *History of the Girondists*, and write a French verb. Then I take half an hour's quick walk; read letters and answer them. From half past eleven till twelve write French. From twelve until one read Girot's *Life of Cromwell*. Ride until five. Read *Life of Charles I* until six. Dine. In the evening read the newspapers.

Tuesday 16 May: London

Last night I went to Lady Bellingham Graham's party. Stupid and bad. Cambridge I have now almost forgotten, and only think of with a sigh of regret. Here I am leading exactly the same idle, useless life as usual in London. Unable to settle anything. I do not like to think of the time when the season will have ended. It is such a perilous time for men's hopes and prospects. How different my foreign journal reads to this disjointed, stupid string of complaints – and this is pleasure!

Tuesday 23 May

Went last night to Lady Antrobus' concert. It was instrumental, the rooms crowded and impossible to hear, so at 11.00 I went on to Lady Louisa Pennant's. I danced with Miss Selina Ramsden, Miss Bathurst, Lady Gertrude Douglas and Miss Pennant. Annesley came late and I walked home with him at 3 o'clock. He had been all the evening listening to a great debate in the House, and talking about it made me feel the emptiness and folly of an evening spent like mine; sheer folly; dancing with ugly girls I have known these five years. I came home quite resolved not to make such a business of society, but to take it calmly.

28 May 1854

Dined last night with Lord and Lady Bennedale: a stupid and bad dinner. I sat beside Miss Hogg who was very pleasant. Went on to a ball at Mrs Talbot Clifton's, but only stayed a few minutes. From there to Lady Louisa Douglas Pennant's ball which was delightful. Lady Lucan very gracious; she really looks into one's eyes so that you do not know what to do; as usual a few questions as to my prospects, all dropped quite casually and in the prettiest way imaginable. Everybody so charming. Lady Loudes is becoming desperate; what shall I do? She dragged me down to supper. At any rate her shrewdness fixing her regards on me indicates a rise in social thermometer. Lady Lucan and she are as good as a farce.

31 May (Derby Day)

Dined at home; feeling rather depressed at thinking of all the excitement and enjoyment going on around me, while I sit solitary in these vast gloomy rooms. How curious it is to look at our family party, lying gloomy and querulous each in their arm chair by the fire; and think of the wealth and position that fortune has lavished upon us, and how little we enjoy it. Splendid to relate, very little in reality. What an odd young man I am.

Tuesday 12 June

Went to the Fitzwilliams' ball. The house very handsome indeed, especially the ground floor, but crowded to excess with Yorkshire, Northamptonshire and Irish people. I danced with little Miss Lascelles, Lady Jane Grosvenor, Alice Egerton. I was particularly bored and weary. Standing in the hall I went through some most scornful glances from the Lascelles and De Burgh families. What one does go through in London in a day. Such crushing slights and glances; and then to see Jervaise Smith dancing with the most magnificent people; and Bateson smiled upon by that lovely Lady Mary Yorke. It is forced upon one's mind every moment that one is stupid, ugly, slow, foolish-looking, not rich enough to be

worth anyone's while looking after; hated by young men, by all pretty girls: sensitive and perceptive to an almost painful degree.

3 November: Sledmere

I have been very busy today and yesterday framing and hanging prints, my mind absorbed in it and in the arrangement of my sitting-room. These joys, reading in the morning (mostly Dante, Boccaccio, etc.), little things, papers, letters, etc. in the evenings, are very sweet and quiet. The uncongeniality of people around me is my only drawback, and can imagination fancy greater uncongeniality?

15 January 1855: Sledmere

A beautiful day. Rode with Elizabeth on our never-varying ride, and then walked in the walks. Dinner becomes more insupportable every day. Shall I long stay here? I delight in the morning and in the part of the evening I spend in my own room.

18 January

A very cold, snowy day. My wayward spirit rebels more and more every night against the tone that pervades this house among the male portion at least. It is my own fault, but every word, every look raises a spirit of anger and opposition in my mind. I begin to look forward to my visit to London rather, then think of the cold, the scarcity of good eating and drinking, the murky, foggy, dusty, expensive hotel, the waiting for Annesley, the dining clubs, etc. etc., and my spirit sinks back in comparative resignation.

At the end of this particular journal there is a set of rules written on the back cover. They remind Christopher, amongst other things, to attempt to regard society not as a business but as a relaxation, and to have more self-respect, both of which, judging from the later entries, he was to fail to do. The journals continue with an amusing description of his presentation to the Queen.

12 May 1855: London

Yesterday I was presented to the Queen at the levee by the Duke of Cleveland. Ramsden took me in his brougham. It was the most crowded levee since the Queen's accession. From the foot of a very shabby, dingy staircase, thro' a suite of equally dingy old-fashioned rooms, was one dense crowd of struggling uniforms. There were Dukes in stars and garters, 2nd lieutenants, Indian officers, Hindu princes, Crimean heroes without legs and arms, several highland chiefs, hugely fat clergymen; and my own head rising far above all others, decorated with a tinge of orange and black from having been up till nearly four the previous night at Lady Louisa Pennant's. At last, standing between two windows, the diamonds of the Queen's head-dress appeared. It was very awful. I trembled with alarm as I saw the line in front bending low before her; and those who were presented kneeling till their foreheads almost touched the ground. I am only conscious of Lord Breadalbane reading to the Queen – 'To be presented, Mr Christopher Sykes' – and of a horrid kneel in which my sword tilted up against my arm; some diamonds either on the Queen's hands or arms; of entirely overlooking Prince Albert standing by her side; and then of walking out of the room with head cast down and an ashamed feeling of having done it vilely.

Elizabeth Beatrice Sykes, Christopher's sister and riding companion,
was the youngest of Great Great Grandpapa's five surviving daughters (one of them had died as a child).
The others were Katherine, Sophia, Emma, and Mary, who was the only one who remained a spinster.

15 June

The London season was in its midst; a very gay week had just ended. I had been greatly in love and much smiled upon by the beauty par excellence, and our names had been in every old woman's mouth. There had been a quarrel with the countess *mère*: not allowed to dance together yet warm pressing of the hands in the Lancers, and constant meeting of eye. Other young ladies had become charming and affable; vulgar hostesses had asked me to open their balls with great young ladies. I was deeply engaged in a most delicate negotiation between the greatest, wealthiest English house and a young lord, a friend of mine; I was the confidante; the poor girl looked so pleased. Dinners were numerous in prospect; a ball every night; a dinner at Greenwich with a few great friends was to take place the next day. I was stricken with the mumps and shut up in a dark and dismal room at the top of the house, in a high fever, my throat closed up, my face swollen to ten times its size, suffering excruciating pain; and now here I am, gazing listlessly out the window, languid, feeble and low; nobody to come and see me; a melancholy hurdy-gurdy playing 'Jeanette and Jeanot', and the prospect of an exile to Dover tomorrow for some days.

24 July: Sledmere

Been at Sledmere three days. London and all its excitements, its restless nights and languid days, the forced spirits and haggard face of the evenings, and the pleasant society of friends, the great solace, reward for other annoyances, seems gone like a dream. The air here is deliciously sweet, I go out and inhale it; sweet smells; a blackbird that sings loudly under the window, these are the chief incidents of my life. Last Tuesday, at this hour, I was dining in a gorgeous room at the table of the richest prince in London, golden Westminster.

28 July

Letter from Muncaster asking me to be his best man on Thursday next. I have, I know foolishly, accepted his offer. But I like the whole thing: the journey to London, the being asked to fill so important a part at a grand wedding. I, here so humble an individual.

24 February: Sledmere

I am most ungrateful for my numberless comforts and blessings; but I cannot but feel somewhat low spirited when each paper that I open contains some fresh success, political or social, of Ramsden's, while I live a listless, objectless, luxurious life. Having everything that mere money can obtain, but just stopping at the verge of all active or real life; like a great spoilt child, kept at home and allowed everything but independence. It is my own fault doubtless. When shall I learn the proverb that 'a contented mind is a perpetual feast'? I almost dislike my room itself, and all its trophies of eager and unknowing curiosity-hunting. But I will not complain where I ought to be grateful, and I will try not to make this journal a mere barometer of idle self-tortures, that art in which I am so proficient.

28 November: Sledmere

. . . I must and will combat this foolish watchful jealousy. Why should I annoy myself about what I can have no control over? Oh my education! Perhaps I am my own instructor.

30 January 1859: Sledmere

My reading interrupted by meeting my mother in the hall who told me Robert Bower had sent a message

Sir John Ramsden, another member of Christopher's London set.

by Reid to say there were to be three members of the East Riding, and I was to be the third. My father had received the news with positively expressed displeasure. My dear, unselfish mother and Mary most sanguine. At first I was startled and walked along the yews by the church, much pondering, doubting the reality, melancholy about my health, distressed at the position I hold towards Tatton. The only sweetness to think of the triumph it will give me over friends whom I morbidly conceive to have slighted me.

18 February

I cannot write as usual. My whole train of thought has been upset. My father said quietly at dinner, 'James Walker or Willie Worsley are talked of as third members for the East Riding, and I think Walker would be very suitable.' I was chiefly grieved because my poor mother seemed so vexed, and Mary too; the only two people who really care for me. I am very foolish and know I am like a child that cries for the moon.

Here the journals end, on a note of despondency, with Christopher now aged twenty-eight and well established in fashionable circles, but constantly suffering from guilt about the path along which his life was leading him. As it happened he did not have to wait long to achieve his political ambitions for in 1865, after the death of his parents, he was finally elected to the House of Commons as the member for Beverley. Ironically it was a career that did not bring him the satisfaction he had hoped it would. Though he sat as an MP for twenty-seven years, in all that time he made only six speeches, asked three questions and was remembered for no more important work than carrying through a private member's bill for the preservation of sea birds and their eggs. This earned him the nickname that clung to him for life, 'the gulls' friend'. The reason for his singular lack of success as a politician was simple. His attention, as will be seen, was almost always elsewhere.

In the mid 1860s fashionable society had found a new and golden leader in the young Prince of Wales, Edward, who had been driven into its arms by the refusal of his mother Queen Victoria to give him any useful occupation. Among the many people whom he met on his social rounds was Great Great Uncle Christopher. He was instantly captivated by that 'concentrated lump of amiability'. Christopher was ten years older than the Prince and combined charm and elegance with wit and good conversation, as well as possessing the attractive wisdom of the older man. He also knew perfectly how to bear himself in the royal presence, and how to gauge the royal temperament. In short he made the perfect royal companion, and in no time the two men became firm friends. It was a position that transformed Christopher into one of the most fashionable men in England. No longer did he receive derisory glances for being a mere second son, nor did he have to bow and scrape to obtain cards for balls. Society now flocked to press their invitations upon him, and, as flattery turned his head, the old disillusionment began to disappear. He was set on a path that was to end in disaster.

In addition to finding Christopher an excellent companion, there were less romantic reasons for the Prince's attachment to my Great Great Uncle. He also found him extremely useful. After the death of his father in 1863 Christopher had moved into Brantingham Thorpe, a Jacobean manor house which had been left to him near his constituency at Beverley. This was close enough to Doncaster to be a most convenient place for the Prince to stay while attending the Doncaster races, racing being one of his great passions. Brantingham Thorpe answered all the Prince's requirements, particularly as he loved things done in style, and Christopher saw to that. The travel arrangements were luxurious, with many carriages to convey the guests to and from the station at both ends. The guests themselves were chosen with the utmost care and imagination. If there was a current royal favourite then he or she would be there. If there was some eccentric *nouveau riche* millionaire in whom the Prince had expressed an interest, then he would

This photograph represents the first visit of the Prince of Wales to Brantingham Thorpe in 1869.
From left to right, the group consists of the Duke of St Albans, the Prince of Wales, the Queen of Denmark,
the Princess of Wales and Mr Christopher Sykes. In the background can be seen the photographer's carriage.
(overleaf) Brantingham Thorpe, with all the household turned out for the arrival of the Prince of Wales.

In this photograph of a picnic from the royal yacht, Osborne, the Prince of Wales can be seen in the far right of the photograph wearing a cap, his face turned towards the photographer.

(overleaf) A tea party at Waddesdon, the home of Baron de Rothschild, another of the Prince of Wales' millionaire friends. Christopher is seated to the right of the tea table wearing a dark suit.

It was fashionable in late Victorian times for people to leave photographic 'cartes de visite' at the houses where they stayed.
These are from Brantingham Thorpe: (above) Lord Henry Gordon-Lennox; (opposite, clockwise) Lord Henry Scott, Lord de Lisle,
Lady Londesborough, Lord Londesborough.
(overleaf) Another guest of Christopher's was the famous actress Lily Langtry.

be squeezed in. The food was prepared by the best and most fashionable cooks. After dinner there would be dancing to the finest orchestras, or perhaps the latest forms of gambling. No royal whim was uncatered for, with the result that the Brantingham Thorpe parties were dazzling successes, and the Prince could scarcely have enough. There was no longer any host to compare with 'dear old Xtopher', he used to say. Soon, as well as the racing parties, there were hunting parties and shooting parties, followed by a series of sumptuous entertainments given on any excuse. When the parties increased in size, and Brantingham Thorpe was no longer large enough to accommodate them, Christopher obligingly built extensions.

Swelled by his great success as a host Christopher now became quite carried away, and he took a large house in London, in Hill Street, in which to continue his entertainments during the London season. Naturally this was much to the delight of the Prince who lost no time in taking advantage of it, safe in the knowledge that an evening at Hill Street would never be dull. Equally important, it would be discreet. Before long the Prince was using Hill Street as a sort of free hotel and, whereas royal commands for dinner parties had once arrived at least a week in advance, Christopher was soon lucky to get two days' or sometimes even twenty-four hours' notice – and the commands seemed never-ending. A severe strain began to show on Christopher's income. It was only the beginning of his troubles.

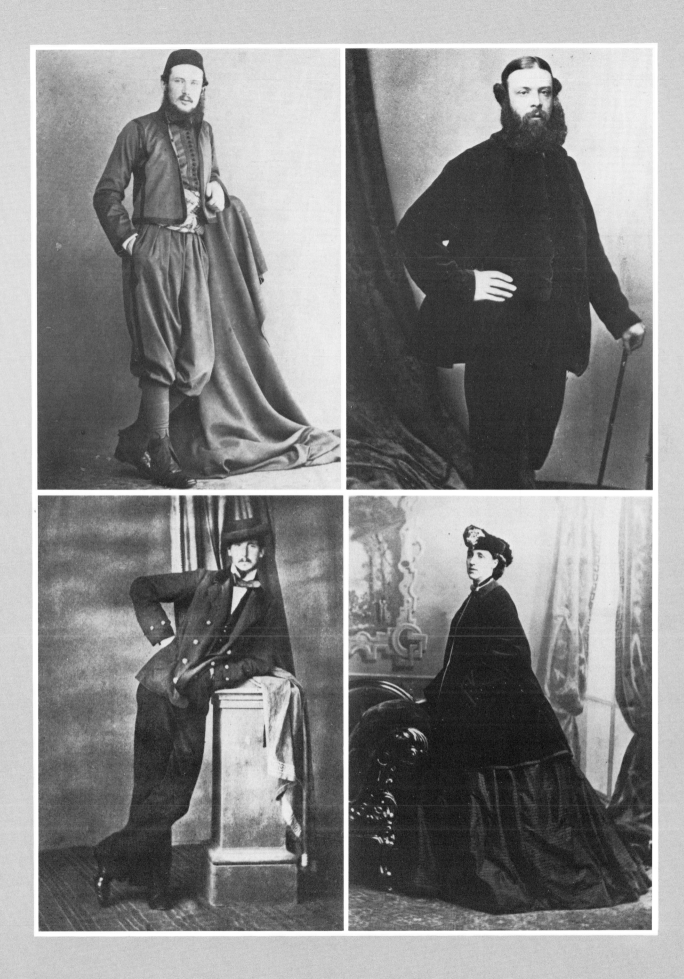

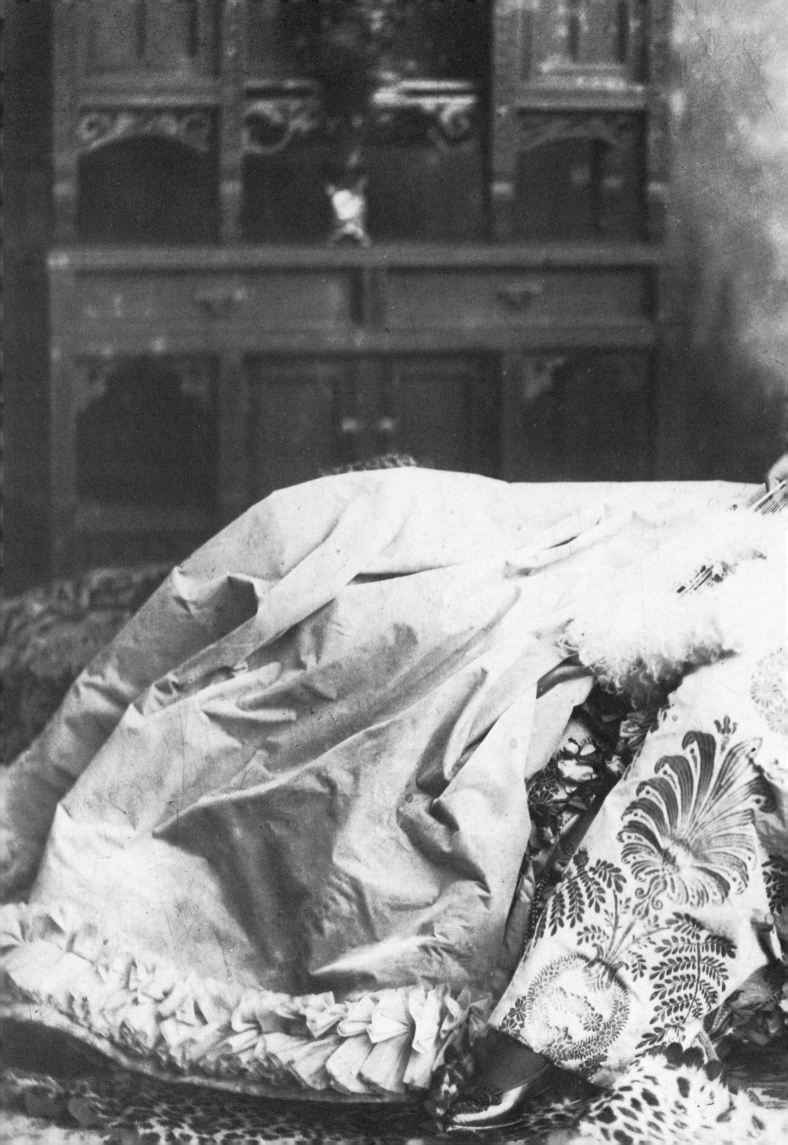

The figure lying at the feet of Jessica, in this group taken at Brantingham Thorpe, is Lord Charles Beresford.
'Charlie', the second son of the Marquis of Waterford, was a very dashing and popular figure
on the social scene after his participation in the bombardment of Alexandria and the Nile expedition in the early 1880s.
(opposite, clockwise) Mr Christopher Sykes, Mrs Standish, Mr Standish, Lord Charles Beresford, Lady Charles Beresford.

The problem with entertaining the Prince of Wales was that he was easily bored, and thus was constantly in need of new diversions. In a way Christopher had rather overplayed his hand. He had given the ultimate in parties and, though they continued to be no less excellent, they began to lose their glitter for the Prince. He looked on Christopher to provide some new form of amusement. This he was to do, but in a quite unexpected way. One evening, during a supper at the Marlborough Club after a late sitting at the House of Commons, Christopher was sitting next to the Prince who, on a sudden whim and without the slightest warning, turned and emptied a whole glass of brandy over his friend's head. My Uncle Christopher takes up the tale:

When the brandy landed on his hair and trickled down his face to the golden beard, Christopher showed a rare thing: an excess of presence of mind. Not a muscle moved. Then, after a pause, he inclined to the Prince and said without any discernible trace of arrogance or amusement, 'As your royal Highness pleases.' The effect of this is recorded as being quite indescribably funny. The whole room burst into violent paroxysms of laughter, and no one laughed more heartily, and certainly not more loudly than the Prince. Laughter begat laughter, the jest was prolonged till the very act of mirth was unbearable. Christopher dripped. Without a smile on his face he made no effort to mop up the tiny rivulets of spirit. The brandy had been poured by a royal hand. It was sacred!

In this attempt to maintain his dignity Christopher had made a fatal mistake, and there was no turning back. The Prince, once he had discovered this new form of entertainment and the apparent effect that it had on those around him, could not be stopped. At the Marlborough Club, at Brantingham Thorpe, at grand houses all over England, glasses of brandy became decanters that were poured over Christopher's head and down his neck; cigars were stubbed out on his hand; games of billiards turned into shrieking rags as he was hurled under the table and speared with cues; and when the old companion was finally allowed to stagger to his bedroom he would find his bed soused with water or filled with objects, on one occasion a live, trussed rabbit, and on another a dead seagull, a particularly cruel jest in the circumstances. And, as my uncle Christopher relates, the ridicule was not confined to private houses:

On one occasion the Prince attended a fancy dress ball. Christopher accompanied him dressed in complete steel. As they approached the house the Prince declared that to avoid making a public appearance in his costume he had arranged for the party to be let in by the back door. It was a plot and it succeeded. As the party entered Christopher found himself last, and, at the moment when he was about to walk in, the door was slammed and locked. He knocked. He knocked many times. As the minutes went by the unusual spectacle began to attract a crowd of curious people. The house into which he so passionately wished to go was one of those immense, round family palazzos whose back door was in a part of London not distant from, perhaps, but not sharing life with, the region in which the front door was situated; so much so, in fact, that the inhabitants of the back door area had not become involved in the excitement in front. They had not heard about it. What they saw was a bright, fully armed man standing in the street. Christopher saw that there was nothing for it: he must walk down the street, turn left up the next street, second right and then left down to the main street, and so left again to the front door. Normally five minutes, six in armour. It is said that when he arrived, the vociferous crowd which he brought with him was large enough to add a good third to the numbers already assembled about the front door. Six minutes in armour can be a very long time!

Two shooting parties: (top) at Wynnard, with Lord Londonderry (seated on the ground, bottom right);
(bottom) at Longleat, with the Marquis of Bath (standing on the right of the group).
(opposite) An early group taken in 1873 on the steps of Blenheim Palace, home of the Duke and Duchess of Marlborough.

There is no question that Christopher in any way enjoyed these humiliations. One only has to look at later group photographs taken by the court photographer to see the expression of profound melancholy and hopeless resignation etched deep into his face. The trouble was that he had allowed it all to go on for too long. He was in so deep that he no longer had the energy to extricate himself, his only contribution to fighting back being the occasional verbal retort that would thrust right home. 'What d'ye take yourself for, Christopher, hey?', the Prince once shouted. 'For your royal Highness's obedient, loyal and most tried servant,' replied Christopher with a solemnity that apparently silenced the Prince for some weeks.

With the dawning of the 1890s disaster struck. Christopher's dwindling income could no longer stand the strain of continual entertaining. For years the bankers had pleaded with him to moderate his spending, but he had failed to take heed of their warnings and now bankruptcy loomed. And where was the Prince in this hour of need? Was he planning to bail out the old friend whose pride had prevented him from admitting that he could no longer afford to obey the royal commands? The answer is that he was not. His association with the Tranby Croft scandal in 1890 (when the Prince was called as a witness in a court case involving illegal gambling and cheating) had made him nervous. He was afraid to get involved. He could only exclaim that it was 'a thoroughly bad business' and continue to hide his head in the sand. But not for long. Glorious intervention came from an unexpected quarter. A certain person was consumed with anger at the way in which Christopher was being treated, a person who was not afraid of

A house party at Chatsworth given by the Duke of Devonshire for the Doncaster races. The Duke is seated on the far left.

*Tranby Croft, 1890. As Christopher's bankruptcy took place shortly before his annual party
for the Doncaster St Leger race meeting, he was obliged to inform the Prince of Wales that, unfortunately,
the party would have to be cancelled. However, at the Prince of Wales' request, he did manage to find accommodation
for them in a neighbouring house, Tranby Croft, as guests of the* nouveau riche *shipping millionaire Arthur Wilson.
It was during this party that the famous card game took place in which Sir William Gordon-Cumming
(standing at the far back, against the door) was accused of cheating,
a scandal which led to the Prince of Wales' appearance in public court as a witness.*

princes; no less a person in fact than Jessica Sykes. Down to London she stormed and to an appointment with the Prince in Marlborough House. There is no record of what was said at this meeting. All that is known is that shortly after it took place Christopher's debts were paid. Thus at the end of the day Christopher was saved from the disgrace of bankruptcy – but at a price. He lost most of his capital, the house in Hill Street and his beloved Brantingham Thorpe.

Christopher spent the rest of his life as an endless guest, a grand, displaced person on a prolonged tour of country houses, an ironical fate for the man who had been the greatest of all hosts. It was a role that did not suit him. He began to decline. Look at the photographs: though still in the circle of royal friends, he is no longer the imposing figure of early days, but a faded and tired-looking old man surrounded by a younger and more glamorous set. To make things worse his health began to fail, the result of too many years of good living, and he began to take yearly cures at Hamburg.

'Reaching the Pyramids at about four we found our tents pitched just where mine was when I was here before; one large tent, and three small ones. We then began the ascent of the great Pyramid. I went alone and very leisurely, and was quite astonished at how soon and how easily I reached the top. All the party, indifferent to the view, began to carve their respective names with all their might. I enjoyed the view, but it was a sadly inferior one to when all the valley of the

Nile was one sheet of water as when I was last here. The Libyan desert was as beautiful as ever, and when the sun set the pale light of the moon had a lovely effect. Coming back to our tents we found a capital dinner ready; a good Irish stew, boiled chicken, champagne and marsala. After dinner we all walked out in the moonlight to salute the Sphinx.'

(Extract from Christopher's diary)

This photograph, taken at Waddesdon in 1894, shows how old and tired Christopher was beginning to look during this period.
(opposite) Christopher asleep on the royal yacht Osborne.

It was while on one of these in 1898 that an unrelated event took place that was to have the most drastic consequences for him. At the time, the Prince of Wales was aboard the royal yacht when he slipped and broke his ankle. The doctors confined him to bed, to him the ultimate boredom. A diversion was needed and he summoned Christopher from Hamburg. When the reply arrived expressing the most profound apologies and begging the royal pardon that he was too ill to come, the Prince angrily sent off a second, more forceful summons. Christopher could refuse once, but never twice, and, even though he knew himself to be on his last legs, he somehow made the painful journey to the royal yacht. His appearance shook even the Prince who is said to have dearly regretted sending that second telegram. Christopher stayed a few days and then begged leave to return home; this time the Prince did not object. He left for England a tired, defeated man, and soon after his arrival there he died.

Great Great Uncle Christopher was buried in Brantingham Thorpe. The Prince did not attend the funeral. It was just as well. When the time came for the coffin to be lowered into the grave it was discovered that, whichever way it was tried, it would not fit. God alone knows what effect this might have had on the royal party, what helpless laughter might have interrupted the sad ceremony. Instead the Prince sent a wreath which bore the inscription, 'In sorrowful remembrance of an old and faithful friend'. For those who wish to see it, there is however a more permanent memorial. In a window in the royal chapel at Sandringham is an inscription which bears witness to the fact that Edward, Prince of Wales once had a deep and lasting friendship for one Christopher Sykes.

Mr Thelwell's Album

Henry Thelwell was the village school master in Sledmere during Great Grandpapa's lifetime. His hobby was photography, and he used it to create a fascinating record of the people who lived and worked in the village.

(above) Mr Thelwell and the Sledmere school band in 1883.
(opposite, above) The vicar, the Reverend A. S. Wilton, and his choir.
(below) Sledmere school group.

The stable-hands. (opposite, top) The woodmen. (bottom) The sawyers.
(overleaf) A group of carpenters in the estate works yard.

(top) Robert Monkman and John Wood, gate painters. (bottom) Jim Wood, the village cobbler.
(opposite) Leonard Clarke, a gardener.

Chapter 5
Great Great Aunt Venetia

HINK OF ALL the good and worthy people there must be who have led good and worthy lives, unselfish to a degree, kind, generous and Christian. Yet when they die, are their deeds recorded for posterity, handed down from generation to generation amid gasps of wonder? Rarely so. As we have seen, it is invariably the extravagant, the tragic, the outrageous who make for good history, for enjoyable ancestors. So with Great Great Aunt Venetia who became a legend in our family, even in her own time, by her fanatical meanness, made all the more extraordinary by the fact that it was concerned not with hundreds of pounds, with which she would willingly part, but with shillings and, even more, with pence. This exaggerated sense of economy had been instilled in her from an early age by her mother, the dominating Brittania, whose husband George Augustus Frederick had failed to inherit a fortune, being only a son of a fourth son of the Duke of Portland, and who was fast on his way to bankruptcy. So deeply embedded was this parsimony that it remained with her for the rest of her life, in spite of her marriage to an immensely rich man.

Arthur James was an American, the eldest of three brothers who had inherited a vast fortune built up since the turn of the nineteenth century, first of all in lumber, then in railways, copper and alarm clocks. He had settled in England, one of the new breed of *nouveau riche* who were springing up all over the country. His marriage to Venetia was not frowned upon by Brittania. He was, like herself, of Irish origins, and his money proved advantageous to them all, for when George Augustus Frederick died leaving endless debts behind him Arthur helped out by buying his London house, 3 Grafton Street. Arthur proceeded to decorate this house, with its pretty Adam staircase, in the most vulgar millionaire style, filling it with marble and gold. In keeping with his new married status he also bought a large country house, Coton near Rugby, so that in no time Venetia found herself mistress of two 'mansions', as she used to call them. To her this was an advantage that far outweighed the disadvantage of being married to Arthur: he was impotent. This was the only thing that ever caused her to step out of line. She had several affairs, but they were always carried on within the framework of society's golden rule: extreme discretion at all times.

Aunt Venetia as a child.

115

Venetia, Jessica and their mother, Britannia, strike a typically sentimental Victorian pose.
(opposite) Aunt Venetia's husband, Arthur James (on the right) was a small and insignificant-looking man. He was also impotent.

Great Great Aunt Venetia lost no time in using her new-found wealth and position to establish herself as one of society's top hostesses. She had a good start. Arthur James, being an American millionaire, had all the qualities necessary for friendship with the Prince of Wales, and by the late 1890s they were firmly established in the Marlborough House circle. Luckily for posterity Arthur must have given Venetia a camera early on in their marriage, for she became a keen photographer and kept a series of albums painstakingly recording their life together. We see the grand houses they visited together in a collection of interior photographs remarkable for their professionalism and eye for detail. There are the inevitable formal groups, such as the top-hatted Doncaster party; but interspersed all the way through are more informal and charming snaps, such as the Prince of Wales' leaping dog, Arthur and his tall friend, Venetia's nieces, and what is probably one of the last photographs ever taken of King Edward and Alice Keppel together in Biarritz before his death. In many houses it was fashionable to keep photographs of guests in the visitors' book, and Coton was no exception. There, alongside the signatures and framed in the most elaborate manner, are the faces of all the friends who passed through. The photographic sessions took place in the conservatory on Sunday afternoons.

Aunt Venetia took this photograph of the drawing room while staying with the Prince of Wales at Sandringham. (opposite) The drawing room at Alloa, home of Lord Mar and Kelly.

Once she had reached her peak as a fashionable hostess Great Great Aunt Venetia was determined to remain there, and she carefully avoided anything that might adversely affect her position in society. Thus she would have nothing whatsoever to do with Jessica whom she considered to have disgraced herself beyond all measure. The last thing she wanted was for any of the dirt to rub off on her. As far as possible her parties were made up of royalty, politicians and ambassadors. Knowing them gave her a feeling of being very close to the seat of power. She never bothered to soft-pedal her snobbery. For example, on one occasion at Coton, after looking round the dining-room table she was heard to exclaim, 'What? Only one baronet and one viscount! What a mangy weekend!' But even her most outrageous snobbery was always superseded by her meanness, and when it came to making an economy all else was forgotten. The Italian ambassador was once staying at Coton for a weekend and, when on Monday he had to return to London, Venetia insisted that he should ride to the station in the butcher's meat van. This would save her the cost of the petrol her own car would have used. A fellow guest, Lady Max Muller, wife of the British ambassador in Poland, thought this was going too far and she stepped in to rescue the poor man. 'Venetia,' she said, 'the ambassador travels in the meat van over my dead body!'

There are countless 'Aunt Venetia stories' in this vein, undoubtedly exaggerated by time, and they cover every conceivable aspect of her life. At times she took her thriftiness to an almost insane degree and upset herself by it. For example, when the first underground railway opened in London she was overjoyed at the amount of money she could save on cabs, and consequently took to using it as often as possible. On the occasion in question a friend of hers was in Dover Street station when he came across a large crowd of people assembled around a ticket machine. There were raised voices emerging from the centre of this crowd, one of which he instantly recognized as Aunt Venetia's. Pushing his way to the front he found her shaking with rage, and screeching at a harassed-looking policeman, 'Officer, I shall not leave until this machine has been taken to pieces. I put my coin in and no ticket came out.' The ticket was only worth a penny! It was the same with the telephone: if somebody rang her up at home when she was otherwise occupied she would keep them hanging on the line until she had finished what she was doing – this could be ages – in order that she did not have to 'waste money' ringing them back.

There seemed to be no area in which her economies were not absurd. Her niece Audrey was one day walking past 3 Grafton Street on the way back from a shopping expedition in Piccadilly, when Aunt Venetia appeared at the front door and said, 'Come in, my child, wouldn't you like a little light refreshment?' Surprised by this unusually generous offer from her aunt, Audrey eagerly accepted the invitation, but was horrified, particularly as she detested cats, when she heard Aunt Venetia shouting to her housekeeper, 'Emily, Emily, if the cat has left any of its milk, bring it up for Mrs Coates.' She could

The main sitting room at Warwick Castle. (opposite) The library at Rufford Abbey.
(overleaf) The winter garden at Moulton Paddocks, home of South African diamond magnate Jack Joel.

not bear to see anything wasted. Once, while taking her daily constitutional in Hyde Park, accompanied by an old diplomatic friend, Sir Charles Degraz, she suddenly turned to him and said, 'Sir Charles, I see a dead sparrow in the long grass beyond the nannies' walk. Do you mind picking it up?' He obliged her and was made to carry the little corpse all the way back to Grafton Street, which he did at arm's length and held delicately between the thumb and forefinger of his gloved hand. When they arrived there, Aunt Venetia shouted down the area steps, 'Emily, Emily, discommand the cat's meat. Sir Charles has brought her a fallen bird.'

When it came to private entertaining Aunt Venetia was equally fastidious. Where she could, she would persuade her butcher to allow her to take meat on sale or return, which explains why she could be seen walking down Bond Street carrying a terrible, greasy parcel: it would be bacon she was returning after the weekend. As for leftovers, these were never allowed to be thrown away, and her cook's imagination would be stretched to its limits as to how to re-use them. On Friday nights she would try and include as many Catholics as possible at her dinner parties for she knew that they had to be served fish and, being cheaper than meat, it would of course help cut down the food bills. 'Fish for the papists!' she would hiss

The hall at Coombe Abbey. (opposite) The staircase at Highcliffe Castle.

as the other guests helped themselves to meat. When meat was being served to the whole party the servants were instructed to keep helpings to a minimum. On one celebrated occasion, when a single chicken had been eked out to serve about ten people, she was seen to pass a note to her butler, Went, which read somewhat mysteriously 'DCSC'. It was a code which, when cracked, turned out to mean 'Don't Cut Second Chicken'.

Guests staying for a summer weekend at Coton were considerably luckier than those invited in mid-winter. Married couples and ladies were allowed only one fire in their bedrooms, a rule which prompted Alice Keppel to tell Aunt Venetia quite sharply, 'Venetia, I am paying your maid £1 a day never to let my fire go out.' As for the poor bachelors, fires in their wing were strictly forbidden. It is hardly surprising, therefore, that guests would often come down before dinner to find pairs of pyjamas airing in front of the drawing-room fire!

Aunt Venetia's nieces at Coton: Sandra, Sylvia and Audrey.
(opposite) A paddling party.

One may well wonder why, if she was so mean, people bothered with Aunt Venetia at all. The answer is that in the end they began to find it funny. It became almost a game to see who could tell a new 'Aunt Venetia story'. Violet Trefusis, for example, had her own favourite in which Aunt Venetia, rather than being ridiculed, came out as rather a witty figure. Her god-daughter was the present Queen Mother and, when she became engaged to the Duke of York, Aunt Venetia decided to give a weekend party for them. For this special occasion she went out and bought a new hat, spending more than she usually would on such a purchase. With the hat fixed firmly on her head, and accompanied by Violet, she then went off to Euston to catch the train to Coton. When she got there, however, it was to find that the fast, direct train had only first-class carriages, and Aunt Venetia naturally never travelled first-class – 'a *ridiculous* waste of money', she used to say. Eventually she found a train with the required third-class compartments and, despite the fact that travelling on it necessitated a change halfway, she boarded it, dragging Violet behind her. They soon found themselves standing on the platform of some small station in the Midlands waiting for the train to Rugby, when there was a sudden cloudburst. Without any hesitation Aunt Venetia lifted her skirts and her red flannel petticoats and held them over her head. At this point the station-master appeared and, walking up to Violet, said, 'Can you please tell that lady she can't stand like that. It's indecent.' When Violet replied that she didn't know 'that lady', he approached Aunt Venetia directly and repeated, 'Madam, you shouldn't stand like that. It's indecent.' Through the layers of red flannel came back Aunt Venetia's voice: 'My good man, what you see is old but the hat is new.'

Spontaneous outbursts of wit such as this leave one in no doubt as to how sharp her mind was. There were other indications of it too. Every morning at Coton Aunt Venetia would lead the household in prayers. A gong would be rung at about 8 a.m. and all the servants would file into the dining-room – the butler, the first and second footmen, the man who cleaned the billiard room, the cook, the first and second kitchen maids and the scullery maid – and they would sit down solemnly on a long row of Chippendale chairs, while all around them portraits by Romney and Reynolds stared down from the red damask walls. Aunt Venetia then took her place at the head of the long mahogany dining-table, and read the gospel and the collect for the day. For the family, like the servants, attendance at prayers was compulsory. Guests, on the other hand, were not obliged to attend. On this particular occasion, however, Victor Cazalet thought he would get into Aunt Venetia's good books by coming down to join the service. Unfortunately for him he was late, and arrived almost as prayers were over. As if this was not enough he also let in Wong, one of the chows, who immediately set about sniffing round the praying bottoms. All this infuriated Aunt Venetia and that morning the Lord's Prayer went as follows: 'Our Father, who art in heaven, who let Wong in? My kingdom come, thy will be done on earth as it is in heaven. Give us this day our daily bread. If you're coming in, come in, and forgive us our trespasses. Aren't you going to kneel down you fool?!' A similar occurrence took place after my Aunt Freya, as a

The Prince of Wales (George V)'s children, 1903: (left to right) Prince Henry, Prince Albert, Princess Mary, and Prince Edward. (opposite) Millicent James, another of Aunt Venetia's nieces. (overleaf) Peter, the Prince of Wales' leaping dog.

child, was late for prayers. She remembers Aunt Venetia saying, 'Our Father, who art in heaven . . . GO AWAY!'

This daily holding of prayers does not mean that Aunt Venetia was a very religious person, at least in the sense of having a deep love of the Holy Spirit. She believed in the afterlife and, to her, prayers, together with regular attendance at church on Sundays, were like paying premiums to get into heaven. When her 'mansion' in Grafton Street was bombed during the last war, it was on a Sunday and she was out at church. A great bronze chandelier fell through the ceiling and smashed to pieces the *boule* table, at which she used to conduct her business each morning, and the gilt Louis XIV chair in which she used to sit. When she returned and saw the devastation, all she said was, 'At last my piety has been rewarded!'

Aunt Venetia lived to a ripe old age, surviving Arthur by thirty years, and during all that time neither her thrift nor her social life diminished. In fact, right into the late 1930s, she still minded desperately

Edward VII and Alice Keppel, his mistress, photographed in Biarritz shortly before his death.
(opposite) The Coton visitors' books were illustrated by Aunt Venetia with delightful collages,
such as this one of a Christmas houseparty. (overleaf) Two more pages from a Coton visitors' book.

about which parties she was or was not invited to. Weekends at Coton remained a routine, and when most of her contemporaries had faded away she filled the house with her nephews and nieces. For them, however, these parties do not hold such glittering memories since Venetia was never especially indulgent to the young. Instead, it is the incidents that made them laugh which stand out. The time, for example, that Aunt Venetia's chow, Wong, killed a sheep and she burst into tears. They were tears shed, not for the dead sheep, but for the awful cost of replacing it. Or the day that the vet came to attend the dogs and,

while he was there, Aunt Venetia was told that one of her maids was ill and needed a doctor. 'A doctor!' shrieked Aunt Venetia; 'A ridiculous waste of money! The vet can see to her.' Then there was her passion for motoring which she indulged at great risk to the life and limbs of others. She drove at reckless speed, always looking over her shoulder. In the end after she had once turned over the car, she so terrified Went that he refused to travel with her anymore. There were incidents too that show how her mind used to wander at times. Went entered the library one day to find Aunt Venetia sitting in an armchair reading a rather crumpled-looking newspaper and muttering to herself, 'I simply don't understand this paper. I'm sure I've read about this somewhere before, unless the same thing's happened twice. Most extraordinary!' 'Madam,' said Went, 'you are reading the paper off which the dog has eaten its dinner!'

When Aunt Venetia died, aged eighty-four, the world had not heard the last of her. Some time after her death Lord Berners and a friend of the James family called 'Bogey' Harris were walking down Wigmore Street late one evening when they passed a large notice outside the Wigmore Hall advertising a meeting of the International Spiritualists' Society which was taking place there, and to which the public were invited. Thinking they would have a good laugh they bought seats, little realizing the shock they were in for. As they entered the gallery the meeting was already in progress, and on the darkened stage there stood one of the world's leading mediums, illuminated by a single spotlight. Hardly had Bogey and Lord Berners sat down when she said, 'Is there a Mr E. L. Harris in the hall?' These were indeed Bogey's initials and Lord Berners, pushing him up to the front, told him to own up. Leaning over the balustrade, and with a lump in his throat, Bogey raised his hand and said, 'I am Mr Harris.' The medium raised her eyes towards the gallery. 'Did you know a Mrs Arthur James who has passed beyond?' When he admitted somewhat breathlessly that he had, she continued, 'Are you prepared to receive a message from Mrs Arthur James?' He nodded his head, and the message rang out across the hall as follows: 'Mrs Arthur James wishes you to tell her butler Went that she is waiting for him.'

133

Next Day is
1901.

Sudley.   Jan 1st — 7th.

Rosie James   Jan. 3rd — 5th.

David Bailey.   Jan " 4th
Villiers   Jan 3rd — 7th.

Dorothy Holyar.   Jan 4th — 7th.

Violet Savile   "   "

Celia Goff   "   "

Mary Bentinck   Jan 4th — 7th

Rupert Guinness   Jan 4th — 7th

Ronald Hamilton   " 5th — 7th

H Spender Clay   5th — 7th

Walter S. M. Burns   "   "

Herbert   "   "

135

Chapter 6
Grandmama Lily

WHEN I CONSIDER Grandmama Lily's parentage the bizarre events that befell her in her early years somehow seem less of a surprise. She was the daughter of a woman who was herself involved in one of the most notorious scandals of the Victorian era, Lady Florence Paget, better known as the 'Pocket Venus'; perhaps the most outstanding beauty of her day, her 'petite figure and dove-like eyes' had made her 'the rage of the park, the ballroom, the opera and the croquet lawn'. Shortly before her intended marriage to Henry Chaplin, a prominent society figure and an intimate of the Prince of Wales, she had caused a sensation by eloping with the Marquis of Hastings, a notorious rake, after a rendezvous in the unlikely surroundings of that celebrated London store, Marshall and Snelgrove. For having thrown aside her fiancé for a man with greater riches and a title, as society saw it, she was branded as a worthless and despicable woman and never forgiven. If she had believed that by marrying this rake she could reform him and turn him into a young man of whom she could be proud, then she was sadly mistaken. Harry Hastings, 'the Wicked Marquis', drank and gambled his life away. In 1868, after a marriage of four years and three months, the Pocket Venus found herself a widow at the age of twenty-six. Within a year and a half of Harry's death from 'a disease of the kidneys', Florence, whose loneliness was worsened by being given the cold shoulder by society, married again. Perhaps she saw herself as a salvationist, for her second husband was also a compulsive gambler. He was Sir George Chetwynd and he was, wrote George Lambton in his memoirs, 'more talked of, more envied and, in some quarters, more disliked than any man of the fashionable world'. But success as a reformer sadly eluded Florence, for she failed with George Chetwynd as she had with Harry Hastings, and consequently her life with him was not a very happy one. She did however bear him four children, one son and three daughters, and it was the eldest of these daughters, Lilian Florence Maud, who was to become my Grandmama.

Lady Florence Paget, the 'Pocket Venus', and the mother of Grandmama Lily. She was the most famous beauty of her day and became notorious for her elopement with the Marquis of Hastings.

Harry Hastings, the 'Wicked Marquis'. He drank and gambled his life away.
(opposite) Henry Cyril Paget, 5th Marquis of Anglesey. (inset) Coquelin, the French actor of whom he was the illegitimate son.

Grandmama Lily was born with bright red 'Titian' hair, which her mother considered an obvious sign of a weak character. Determined therefore that her daughter should not get into the same kind of trouble as she had, at the earliest possible moment Florence arranged for Lily to marry her first cousin, Henry Cyril Paget, 5th Marquis of Anglesey. It would be, she firmly believed, a safe and respectable marriage. This young man was the great grandson of the legendary 'One-leg' Uxbridge, who had been Wellington's right-hand man at Waterloo and who, when his right knee was shattered by almost the last cannon shot in the battle, had undergone the amputation of his leg without anaesthetic 'without flinching and without complaint'. He was described by contemporaries as 'the most perfect hero that ever breathed'.

Had Henry Cyril had any of his great grandfather's blood then perhaps all would have been well. He did not, however, for his birth was the result of an affair his mother had had with the French actor Coquelin, a notorious womanizer. After his mother died young, Henry Cyril was brought up from the age of two by Coquelin's sister, as a result of which he spent most of his formative years abroad and in the company of theatrical people, which accounted in large part for much that was foreign in his appearance and tastes. He was a delicate, over-sensitive child who, having no brothers and sisters, kept more than

the usual store of birds and animals upon which he could lavish his affections. He learned to lose himself in a world of fantasy by continually dressing up in the theatrical costumes that were always at hand. Henry's trouble was that, lacking the company of other children and spending all his life with actors, the gap between his fantasies and reality became narrower and narrower. By the time he inherited his family estates at Plas Newydd on the Isle of Anglesey in 1898 and the marriage to Lily had been arranged, his love for fancy dress had become an obsession.

The wedding of Grandmama Lily and the marquis took place in January 1898 and, though the marquis had little interest in women, preferring to worship himself, he was evidently struck by the beauty of his young wife. Lily was indeed remarkably good-looking. Like her mother she was petite, with a tiny waist. With her delicate, perfectly-proportioned features, her pale-green eyes and bright, red-gold hair she seemed to have stepped straight out of a painting by Rosetti. So golden was her overall colouring that she was nicknamed 'the Goldfish'.

With his newly acquired fortune and the inspiration of Lily's beauty, Henry Cyril now began to let his fantasies run wild. He started on a new and extravagant craze. With the help of a Polish jeweller, Morris Wartski, whom he established in a shop in Llandudno, he set about the creation of a remarkable collection of jewellery. His passion knew no bounds. It is said that he took Lily to Paris on their honeymoon, and that when she stopped to admire the window display of Van Cleef and Arpels, he bought the entire display for her. He later reduced her to tears by forcing her to wear it all to the races. Within two months of inheriting the estates he had mortgaged his life interest in them as well as in certain policies of life insurance to various bankers, in order to secure £100,000 for the purchase of more and more precious stones. Nothing escaped his notice. Soon there was not a jeweller in Europe who did not know that if he acquired some particularly rare and fine gem, he would almost certainly find a buyer in the Marquis of Anglesey.

Grandmama Lily left the marquis after precisely six weeks of marriage and almost immediately started nullity proceedings against him. Most of what happened during those six weeks remains a mystery, but whatever it was it was bad enough to make Lily wish to blot out the memory of it altogether, just as if the marriage and all that had gone with it had never existed. She spoke to no one about it, and few dared ask, as one of her closest friends Lady Morisson-Bell remembers: 'I had lots of ideas, when I used to see her hairbrushes with Lily and the coronet on top of them, of wanting to ask her, but I just felt I couldn't. I don't think she would have let one.' She was right. One friend who did broach the subject in later, happier years, Jo Churston, received the reply, 'Once you've sailed your boat into the harbour, Jo, you don't take it out again.'

There is one fact, however, which sheds some light on what the young and inexperienced Lily was thrown into from her previously sheltered life. Each night her husband made her undress, and he would then cover her naked body in jewels until she stood before him dripping in emeralds and diamonds. She was then forced to sleep wearing those jewels. In view of this it is hardly surprising that in later years she developed an obsessive hatred of jewellery and only ever wore strings of heavy amber beads.

When Lily left him the marquis immersed himself in theatricals. He began by converting the chapel at Plas Newydd, now grandly renamed Anglesey Castle, into a theatre, which he modelled after Sarah Bernhardt's in Paris. Called the Gaiety it was decorated throughout in white and blue, and closely packed it was capable of holding about 150 people. The organ loft he turned into a private box for his own use.

Plas Newydd saw many changes under the rule of the 'Dancing Marquis'. It was grandly renamed Anglesey Castle, extravagant parties were thrown there, and the chapel was turned into a theatre.

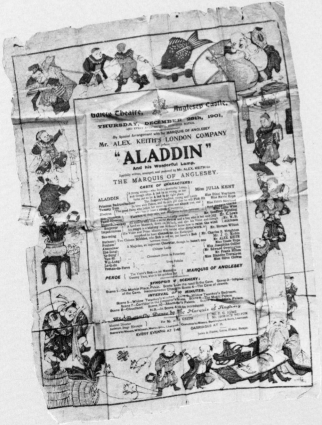

The Dancing Marquis in one of his favourite roles as Queen Eleanor, complete with moustache!
(opposite) Grandmama Lily in her robes as the Marchioness of Anglesey.

He commissioned a London company, that of Mr Alex Keith, to open the theatre formally with a production of *Aladdin*. The role of Pekoe 'the vizier's son, a bit mooney on Yummy-yum' he played himself, in a series of costumes that were the subject of much comment. One was a tightly-fitting suit of white cloth, with a cloak lined with pale salmon-pink silk, and garters, necklaces, rings and other ornaments ablaze with turquoises and diamonds. The jewels on one costume alone were estimated at over £40,000, and it is said that those used in the whole production were worth about half a million.

At a given point during each of these shows the marquis would take over the stage completely for the performance of 'the Butterfly Dance', an act of his own invention that he had previously performed and perfected before the public of Berlin. Now the 'Dancing Marquis', as he was to be forever known, fluttered for an audience drawn largely from his tenants and local shopkeepers. Admission was free.

Inspired by his own performances at the Gaiety and the enthusiastic reception from the local audiences, nothing now could hold back the Dancing Marquis. Firmly convinced that his talents should be shared with the world he financed a series of tours for Mr Keith and his company, which had been elaborately equipped for this purpose. They travelled with specially painted scenery, their own orchestra, and many of their props were exact copies of furniture from Anglesey Castle. For his own use and that of his personal staff of four men the Dancing Marquis had 'a handsomely-fitted motorcar, to say nothing of a fabulous amount of luggage and the case containing his jewels'. When the company was assembled it consisted of fifty people and five truck-loads of baggage and scenery.

Although the Butterfly Dance was performed whenever possible, the programmes on these tours were by no means restricted to *Aladdin*. Other favourites were *The Marriage of Kitty* in which the Dancing Marquis 'was admitted by some capital critics to be distinctly good', and *The Ideal Husband*, a part that 'might have been written for him he went through it so naturally'. From time to time he would appear under a pseudonym. When the company played the Central Theatre, Dresden, a newspaper read:

In the Central Theatre last Sunday, a new artist appeared under the name of 'San Toi'. In a dark house and on a dark stage he produces kaleidoscopic pictures in lifesize. In quick succession San Toi appeared in the costumes of the different nationalities and in all sorts of fancy dress. The splendour and the brightness of the colours, the tasteful combination, and the constant change of the beautiful pictures thrown by electric light on the slender form of the artist, clothed in white, gladdened the eyes. The likeness of the German emperors, William I, Frederick III and William II, of the German heroes of the last decades, and of the Saxon royal couple were beautifully rendered. The production was without any flaw, and was received with great applause. The artist himself is a most interesting personality. He is Lord Anglesey, an English marquis, the head of a noble and well-known English family with a seat and a vote in the House of Lords.

Needless to say the expense of these tours was enormous, and the Dancing Marquis soon got deeper and deeper into hopeless insolvency. The crash came in June 1904 when his trustees took over all his property in order to raise money to pay off the huge list of creditors. The liabilities involved amounted to a staggering £255,969 most of which was owed to jewellers; for instance £26,651 to Morris Wartski, £40,200 to Goudstikker and Son, £31,080 to Haartad Devos, Brussels, and £21,300 to Dobson and Sons. The results of these purchases were discovered by the trustees in large trunks in the attics of Anglesey Castle. When opened these revealed a pirate's treasure of pearls, emeralds and diamonds, innumerable gold cigarette and cigar cases, many of them beautifully studded with the finest diamonds

The Dancing Marquis in one of his most extravagant costumes.
It was said that the jewels on this costume alone were worth over £40,000.

The Dancing Marquis in a bizarre selection of fancy dress.

and rubies, 200 gold scarf pins, plain and jewelled, and, what was perhaps the most remarkable item of all, a magnificent twenty-two foot long chain of gold and precious stones, to which, at intervals of about an inch, were attached hundreds of charms in gold and antique silver.

There followed the great Anglesey sales in which these jewels and the rest of the marquis' personal effects were dispersed. So vast was his accumulation of these that the sales took over forty days, during which 17,000 lots were auctioned, including anything of conceivable value from pedigree dogs to motor cars. The sale of his clothing alone took three days. When the sales were over the Dancing Marquis left the country for France, from whence he was never to return. The following year, after suffering two bad attacks of pleurisy, he died at the Hotel Royale in Monte Carlo. He was thirty, and a bankrupt in the capital of extravagance. There is an interesting postscript. He apparently did not die forgotten by his wife for, according to a newspaper report of the time, when the seriousness of his condition was revealed, the Marchioness of Anglesey was summoned to his bedside and remained with him until he died.

This curious death-bed vigil is only one of the things that reveal something of the enigmatic side to Grandmama Lily's character. Although so disgusted and horrified by the Dancing Marquis that she was driven to leaving him after a mere six weeks of marriage, she withdrew her divorce petition at the last moment and continued to call herself Lady Anglesey. She renounced all the jewels he had given her, yet continued to keep on her dressing table, right to the end of her days, a set of hairbrushes, hand mirrors and little silver boxes, all of which bore huge Anglesey coronets and which must have been a constant reminder of her previous life. Whatever reason she may have had for wishing to hang on to some memory or other, she kept it to herself. She only ever gave the impression that she wished to forget. Certainly the little that is known about her life in the years immediately after she had left the Dancing Marquis bears all the traces of an attempted exorcism.

She moved into a house in London, in Ovington Gardens where, said a friend, 'she dabbled in clever people – actresses, artists and the like'. The bohemian society of the early 1900s was the perfect escape for her, though nobody could move in that twilight world without gossip starting to flow. She was soon said to be receiving numerous lovers, sometimes as many as two or three a night. The flames were fanned even harder by her frequent visits to Paris, a city then notorious for its liberal attitude to loose living, and where, according to the tales that filtered back to London, Grandmama Lily used to sip champagne from slippers and dance on tables.

How much truth there may or may not have been in these rumours, they endowed Lily with a notorious reputation. When in 1909 she announced her intention to marry the son of an eminently respectable family of bankers, who was seven years her junior, it is less than surprising that his family were horrified. John Francis Grey Gilliatt had all the attributes of the eligible bachelor: charm, elegance, wealth, good looks, as well as being a brilliant musician and an all-round sportsman. After giving him the perfect upbringing for a gentleman, a life filled with cricket and tennis weekends, shooting parties and amateur theatricals, the last thing his family had in mind for him was a marriage to an older woman of questionable virtue. This is where Grandmama Lily showed great strength of character. The more the Gilliatt family pleaded with her to leave their Jack alone, the more determined she became to prove to them that they were wrong about her. She married Jack in December 1909, and it was no hardship for her to play the role of an adoring wife. Dropping the title of Lady Anglesey, she now concentrated her attentions on attaining respectability in the eyes of society. It was a hard struggle. Lady Morrison-Bell remembers well how deeply shocked people were when she became a friend of Lily's. 'You shouldn't go near that woman,' they would say, 'you can't touch pitch without catching some smear.' On one occasion Lily and Jack attended a party given by Lady Evylyn Guinness at which the guests of honour were King George V and Queen Mary. Lady Evylyn later received a letter from the King and Queen in which they thanked her profusely for the party, but added, 'We did not enjoy meeting Mrs Gilliatt.'

When Lily realized that the gossip would never stop, she ceased to care. As far as she was concerned she had turned her back on the past as soon as she had married Jack. She set about losing herself in a new life with a set of younger friends who knew nothing of her history. Jack, who was a director of Broadwood's, the piano makers, loved to move in musical circles, and both he and Lily had a flair for the theatrical. Together they soon became well known for the help they gave to struggling young musicians and entertainers. The pattern was always the same: they would throw a party in honour of some young talent whom they particularly admired, to which they would invite, among others, some of their influential theatrical friends such as H. M. Tennant; their protégé would then be expected to play or sing for his or her supper. In this way the word was spread. One of these young hopefuls was Noël Coward. Jack, who presented himself as a rather flamboyant 'actory' figure, with his slightly too large bow ties and his hat always cocked at an angle, was also something of an entertainer, and Lily loved to show him off, making him sit down at the piano after dinner to sing. His most popular number went as follows:

My God she was fat!
She weighed twenty stone in nothing but a hat.
Just fancy that!
My God she was fat!

John Francis Grey Gilliatt, a charming and eligible bachelor who fell head over heels in love with Lily.

Jack and his parrot sitting in the garden of Stragglethorpe Hall where he and Lily lived after the war.
(opposite) Jack and Lily shortly after their marriage.

It did not take Grandmama Lily long to win over the Gilliatt family. She made herself the perfect wife for Jack, and an adoring mother to their three children Simon, John and Virginia. In fact, to the sisters Lydia and Denise (later the Duchess of Bedford and Lady Ebury), who remembered visiting them as children, Jack and Lily's family were almost too good to be true. 'We used to have turbulent fights between ourselves, and so to see Lily and Jack and Virginia and John and Simon never being anything but excruciatingly charming at all times . . . you just felt you longed for somebody to say "Oh bugger you!", or something like that, angrily!' This excessive charm and politeness was a manifestation of the protective shell that Lily had built around the happiness which she had at last found, and which she was utterly determined never to lose. Her feet left the ground and rarely returned there. There is no better reflection of this idyllic life than in Grandmama Lily's family albums whose photographs portray beautifully the bliss of post-First World War summers.

Lily driving with Noël Coward, a friend and protégé of Jack's.
(opposite, top) A summer game of badminton.
(opposite, bottom) Lily's children, John, Simon, and Virginia, playing in a hay field.

Simon and John, who died within eight years of each other. (opposite) Lily's daughter Virginia who was to become my mama.

Of all my grandparents Lily was the only one who lived long enough for me to have known her, and by then she was an old lady in her seventies and eighties, small and fragile as china, and I too young to be interested in her history. She lived in an ugly, pink-stuccoed villa in Sunningdale called Cooralie which Jack had bought during the war so that she would be safely out of London, away from the bombing. Here the only reminders of her early life were the coronetted hairbrushes and a magnificent lifesize portrait of her as the Marchioness of Anglesey, whose cascading red hair and green eyes I fell in love with, and around whose neck there hung an emerald and diamond necklace that stretched to her ankles. By the time I knew her the days of bliss had long since gone and her life had been marred by tragedy. She had worshipped her sons as she worshipped Jack. They were both killed. Simon, a pilot officer in the RAF, was burned to death in August 1936 when his plane crashed on take-off at Farnborough in Hampshire. John, who was also in the plane, was thrown clear and though severely injured made frantic efforts to rescue his brother, but all to no avail. Eight years later he too died while attending a service at the Guards Chapel in London during which it was bombed. When Lily heard the news, Denise Ebury remembers, 'she let out a long, drawn-out groan of despair that I shall never forget.' As if all this were not enough, within four years Jack was gone. After playing a particularly fine stroke, perhaps his best ever, he dropped dead on the golf course.

Lily ended her days at Sledmere, Virginia, her only surviving child, having married my father Richard during the war. It was here that she was brought when it was considered no longer possible for her to remain in Cooralie, even with a companion to look after her, and it was here that she died and was buried among the Sykeses.

Chapter 7
Grandpapa Mark

ON THE OCCASION of his confirmation Grandpapa's friend and tutor Alfred Dowling gave him the following advice: 'Unless you strive and fight against circumstances you will grow up a worthless, cruel, hard-hearted, frivolous man.' The circumstances he referred to were, of course, those of his upbringing under the constant shadow of the long and bitter fight between his parents. Grandpapa took it to heart and, because he did so, he grew up to be an utterly unique and delightful man.

Grandpapa was born in London on 6 March 1879 and brought up to Sledmere by Jessica in April. The arrival of Sir Tatton's son and heir gave the village an excuse for great rejoicing, and no celebration was forgotten. A full choral christening service was held in the parish church and special books printed for the occasion were handed out to the congregation. Then, according to a contemporary report, 'at four o'clock in the afternoon Sir Tatton and Lady Sykes entertained above two hundred of the tenantry and their families, in the great library. The splendid apartment was fitted up as a dining-room, long tables being spread from end to end. Having spent a most enjoyable afternoon the company dispersed after drinking the health of and expressing every good wish for the happiness and welfare of the young Mark Sykes.'

The main influence on Grandpapa's early childhood was undoubtedly Jessica, his father being a far more remote figure. She had already staked her claim on him in 1882 when she had had herself and her son rebaptized as Catholics, a move which Sir Tatton apparently chose not to oppose, but which was highly unpopular in Sledmere where there was a strong Methodist population. They had to go to the local town of Driffield to attend mass, and so from an early age Grandpapa knew what it was like to be a member of a minority. The power of sectarianism was something he was never to underestimate.

In the time that Grandpapa spent with his mother, she taught him a great deal. He learned first of all how to stand on his own two feet. Jessica did not believe in cosseting children, seeing no reason why they should be protected from the world. She treated them accordingly as small adults. As soon as Grandpapa was old enough to grasp the meaning of words, she was eager to share with him her great love of literature and the arts. She read him Dickens and Shakespeare, much of which she could quote from

(opposite) Grandpapa Mark; as an only child he learned independence from an early age.

156

memory, and encouraged him to dress up and act out stories and plays. He soon developed a talent for mimicry and caricature which she relished. She also sowed in him the seeds of a sense of history and of ideals. Being much travelled herself, and knowledgeable about European politics, she brought to life for him all the great statesmen and prominent figures of the past, at the same time passing on her scorn of modern politicians, bureaucrats and businessmen, none of whom had any romance.

Although his father remained a rather distant figure, Grandpapa did not lack male company for he found a close friend and confidant in Tom Grayson the groom, who had been at Sledmere since the days of old Sir Tatton. As well as helping to look after his pack of beloved terriers he taught Grandpapa to ride – 'this is t'thod generation Ah've taught ti'ride', he used to boast – and passed on to him all his knowledge of the countryside. He also gave him a strong sense of locality and origins, keeping him entertained for many an hour with his endless tales of local folklore and legend, some of which were true. There was, for instance, the blood-curdling tale of 'Old Coatee', an old woman so called because she was always wrapped round with a leather coat. One day she was found murdered, her body hidden in a well. According to Grayson's account, a man who had been seen coming out of her house was arrested, and he confessed that he had murdered her. A cage was erected at the corner of the road and the wretch was confined in it and kept without food or drink. Every day a huge peck loaf, new and smoking from the oven, was put in front of his cage so the sight and smell might add to his tortures. He lived for over ten days in this horrible condition – and this had happened little more than a hundred years before. Grayson's mother and grandmother both saw the man and testified that his shrieks were terrible.

As far as company of his own age was concerned, being an only child meant that most of Grandpapa's playmates were from the village, and they naturally looked to the young master just as their parents did to Sir Tatton. He thus became used to getting his own way. His favourite games were military ones. The attics at Sledmere were full of old uniforms and muskets, reminders of the days when Sir Mark Masterman Sykes had raised a local force of yeomanry to fight against Napoleon, and Grandpapa had every opportunity to let his imagination run riot. In the park and paddocks he devised elaborate battles with great attention to detail in the working out of tactics and the building of fortifications, developing early a soldier's taste for command. 'Witness the battle of Sledmere church,' wrote a childhood friend of his, the future Lord Howard de Walden, 'which nearly brought about the death of Grayson. The church was nearly completed to stand as Sir Tatton's permanent protest against the religious beliefs of his wife and successors. Mark ordained that the church was to stand the onslaught of the heretics, represented by old Grayson and the twins of Jones, the jockey. After a prolonged seige the heretics attempted to take the outer palisades of the church by escalade, and were repulsed with one casualty. Old Grayson, being eighty, was not of an age to stand a fall from a fifteen-foot ladder.'

When it came to school almost all of Grandpapa's learning was from experience. He did not have the mind of an academic. Of his time at the village school Mr Thelwell the schoolmaster wrote, 'He was not a diligent scholar: he did not concentrate on his work. Book work was drudgery but, having great powers of observation and a splendid memory, he stored a mass of information.' The only schoolroom in which Grandpapa was remotely happy was a self-made one, the Sledmere library. 'I enjoyed', he later wrote, 'an advantage over most of my age in having access to the very large library at Sledmere, and, before I was twelve, I was quite familiar with the volumes of *Punch* and the *Illustrated London News* for many years back.' From these two textbooks he learned more than from any school.

Tom Grayson, who had been at Sledmere since the days of Great Great Grandpapa.
(overleaf) Grayson leads a sledging party for Grandpapa and some of his friends from the village.

Grandpapa in Jerusalem, aged 9, with the man who was destined to be his guide in later years, Isa Kubrusli.
(opposite) From the age of ten till he was fifteen Grandpapa attended Beaumont Jesuit School.

As it was, Grandpapa's general education was of an extremely erratic nature. The reason for this was that at the age of seven he contracted a congestion of the lungs, and the doctors thought it advisable for him to spend part of the year out of England. It being Sir Tatton's habit to travel abroad every year, he started taking Grandpapa on these trips with him, thereby enabling him both to educate his son in the Eastern travel which he loved so much himself, and carry out the doctor's wishes. The result was that although Grandpapa went to Beaumont Jesuit school when he was ten and remained there till he was fifteen, his education during this time lasted for only some months in the year. 'Before I was fifteen', he wrote, 'I visited Assovan which was then almost the Dervish frontier. Then I went to India when Lord Lansdowne was viceroy. I did some exploration in the Arabian desert, enjoying myself barefooted among the Arabs, and I paid a trip to Mexico, reaching there just when Porfirio Diaz was attaining the zenith of his power.' These travels with his father sparked off in Grandpapa what was to be an undying passion for the East. From childhood his eager eyes were turned towards the mysterious biblical lands, which to him always signified holidays, adventure and romance. And it was because these childhood impressions of the Empire were so powerful that he was to resent more than most the changes that were to come about there through European inroads. In 1898 he wrote of 'the weird Druses of Lebanon', whom few schoolboys could name, let alone place. 'When I was a boy of ten, I was taken by my father to their mountain, again when I was eleven, again when I was thirteen, and lastly, five years later, I visited them alone.'

When Grandpapa returned home after his foreign travels during this period, he also saw something of his mother's Mayfair world. She took him with her to restaurants and to the races, as well as to the plays and operas she liked and felt he ought to see. Consequently his growing-up was a hotchpotch of experiences. By the age of ten he had been exposed to far more than most children of his age and he became an object of curiosity to the other pupils at Beaumont. 'He was quite unlike any other boy', wrote his contemporary Wilfred Bowring, 'and most of the other boys certainly thought him eccentric. He took no part in the games, but soon gathered round him and under him all the loiterers and loafers in the playroom and playground.' On his increasingly infrequent returns to the school 'he reappeared laden with curios from the countries he had visited. These curios nearly always took the shape of lethal weapons, most welcome gifts for his school cronies. He returned from the trips with a smattering of strange tongues. He came back full of the habits, customs, history and folklore of the countries he had visited.' Masters and boys alike would flock round him to hear of his travels and experiences. Here his marvellous memory for detail and his expertise at storytelling came into their own, and he liked to regale his listeners while sitting cross-legged before a hubble-bubble.

It is a credit to Beaumont that Grandpapa was allowed to develop his natural talents rather than be forced into things at which he was no good, like games. His exercise books, instead of being filled with Latin vocabulary, told entertaining histories of Virgil and Cicero, illustrated with marvellous caricatures. This was a device which he was to develop throughout his life, using it in all his writing. In the school magazine, the *Beaumont Review*, he published his first literary effort. Entitled 'Night in a Mexican Station', it was based on a trip he had made with his father to Mexico in the winter of 1891–2 and, though he was only twelve when he wrote it, it was on much the same level as his later efforts as a Cambridge undergraduate. The only award Grandpapa ever received in school was the college elocution prize as the orator in *A Hyde Park Demonstration*, a play he wrote himself, and which was such a success that the whole piece was encored.

It was at this stage in his upbringing that, for the first time, the behaviour of his mother really began to affect Grandpapa's life. She was always asking him for money, or begging him to plead with his father on her behalf. He also came to dread her visits to him at Beaumont in case she was drunk, when he would be mortally embarrassed in front of the other boys. 'I can still see old Lady Sykes', wrote a contemporary, Henry Dickens, 'descending on Beaumont like a thunderbolt, entering into tremendous fights with Father Heathcote, the then and equally pugnacious rector.' Jessica was also responsible for Grandpapa losing one of his closest companions when Lady Howard de Walden, a nervous and delicate woman who had been one of Jessica's best friends, was so outraged by Jessica's behaviour that she forbade her son ever to visit Sledmere again. When they parted 'Mark shook hands with me a little ruefully and said suddenly, "If we meet again we shall smile at this. If not, then was this parting well made."' Things came to a head in 1894 when Jessica removed Mark from Beaumont and sent him to an Italian Jesuit school in Monaco, a move of which he wrote, 'The atmosphere of Monte Carlo, it can be imagined, was a peculiar one for a boy of my years. It is quite natural to think of people going there for pleasure, but for study seems rather curious.' After Beaumont he found the Italian school system 'extraordinarily rigid and hard. It was no child's play at Monaco'. After a year he was sent to another school in Brussels, the Institute St Louis, where he also found 'the boys were very much overworked'.

This constant to-ing and fro-ing gave Grandpapa little opportunity to make school any kind of alternative to the home life in which his parents' obsession with one another left them less and less time for him. In the holidays he looked for support to the new tutor whom Jessica had secured for him and who was to remain a lifelong friend. His name was Egerton Beck and together they spent hours in the library browsing through all the discoveries Grandpapa had made there. Among his favourites were Sir Richard Burton's original translation of *Arabian Nights*, the text and notes of which he almost knew by heart, and Marshal Saxe's *Treatise on Fortification*, knowledge of which was to prove more than useful to Grandpapa during the Boer War. Another close ally during this period turned out to be his father's agent, Henry Cholmondeley, whom Jessica had always tried to turn her son against.

The time that Grandpapa did not spend with these two companions he spent with his terriers, which he had been looking after himself since the death of the old stalwart Grayson in the early 1890s. So fond of them that he could not bear to be parted from them, he even took them to the school in Monaco where 'beyond his schoolwork his chief occupation was the care of his foxterriers, of which he took out three and brought back eight!' When he went to Brussels, however, he had to leave them behind at Sledmere and a most unpleasant incident occurred as a result. In 1896 relations between his parents had come to a head as Tatton abjectly refused to pay any more of Jessica's debts. At some point during the winter of that year Tatton, driven into a terrible rage by Jessica, lost all control of himself and, in a vicious attempt to lash out at her through cruelty to Mark, had all the terriers hanged. It was the knowledge of incidents such as this that prompted his first tutor, Alfred Dowling, to say to Grandpapa with astonishment on the

Grayson and the terriers that Grandpapa loved so much.

eve of his departure for the Boer War, 'How it is that you are no worse than you are, I cannot imagine.'

In the Easter of 1897 Grandpapa went up to Cambridge to Jesus College. It was Jessica who had chosen this college and for a reason typical of her. She had originally intended him to go to Trinity, but when she arrived late from a race meeting for her appointment with the senior tutor, explaining, 'I'm sorry to be late but I've been at the Cesarewitch', and he replied, 'Oh, and where may that be?', she was so disgusted with what she considered a blatant exhibition of stupidity that she left his rooms at once and made for the nearest college. This happened to be Jesus. 'I was going to make sure', she explained, 'that my son was not put in the charge of a lunatic.'

At Cambridge his tutor, the Rev. E. G. Swain of King's College, immediately recognized that, while Grandpapa had no interest whatsoever in the drudgery of preparing for exams and the like, here was a remarkable young man who was head and shoulders above most of the other undergraduates in his knowledge of the world and of the things that matter, and who was also excellent company. As such he introduced him to Dr Montagu James, the great writer of ghost stories and then Dean of King's, with whom Grandpapa struck up an instant friendship. Every evening was open house in the rooms of Monty James and in his autobiography he wrote of 'the delirious evenings in which it was perfectly useless to think you could get anything done the moment you saw Mark put a round, enquiring face (into which he would throw the expression of a stage yokel) round the edge of the door'. He would soon be sitting cross-legged on the sofa holding the company spellbound, perhaps with one of his many impersonations, such as a Yorkshire tenant or a Turkish official speaking French, or maybe with a re-enactment of some melodrama he had seen recently, in which he would take all the parts himself. His 'amazing skill' as an actor greatly impressed Monty James. 'Whatever it was,' he wrote, 'there was genius in it.'

For Grandpapa to have led a normal existence at Cambridge was virtually impossible considering that his time there coincided exactly with the climax of his parents' troubles. He was particularly upset by all the cheap publicity that surrounded the court case, and he could hardly bear to discuss it. It certainly could not have been easy for him to have seen his parents exposed to public ridicule, with his mother made out to be a forger and a perjurer, and his father a mean and foolish old man. He also saw the testimonials of his relatives, friends and tutors pitted against one another, as well as having to stand in the witness box himself. Not surprisingly, he failed the preliminary 'Little Go' exam which he was sitting.

When Grandpapa returned to Cambridge after the case, all he really wanted to do was leave the country, a desire in which he was encouraged by Monty James. He decided to embark on a return visit to Palestine and Syria, the scene of so many happy childhood memories. Jessica had the audacity to say that she would willingly agree to the trip so long as he took her and her maid with him! Enraged, he wrote in a bitter letter to Henry Cholmondeley that clearly the only reason his mother wished to have him at Cambridge was to keep him close enough to London so she could come down and 'extort a few shillings or pounds as the case may be, read all the letters she may find in the room and return to London'. He left on his own for Jerusalem from where he set off to travel as far east of the Jordan as possible, and then north up to Damascus through the remote mountainous Druse country of the Hauran. It was a journey that calmed him, and on his return to Cambridge in the Michaelmas of 1898 his spirits were greatly improved.

One of Grandpapa's great passions was military history and so, not surprisingly, one of the men he admired most was Napoleon. At some time he combined his love of dressing up with his great ability as an actor and had himself photographed as his hero.

Edith Gorst, who Grandpapa befriended at Cambridge and who he later married. (opposite) Grandpapa's letters to Edith were brilliantly entertaining and were always preceded by the words 'honoured and well-beloved co-religionist'. (overleaf) 'Jacob's ladder', taken at Castle Coombe Manor, home of Edith's uncle Edward Lowndes. Edith is fourth from the front.

It was during these autumn months that Grandpapa reacquainted himself and was eventually to fall in love with a girl he had previously met at his mother's house in London. She was Edith Gorst, the sister of his mother's former lover Jack. Her father was the MP for Cambridge and Grandpapa often used to visit the family on Sunday afternoons at their home, Howes Close, where he was welcomed into the fold, which was a considerable one. Besides Edith and Jack, who was the eldest, there was a younger brother Harold who was the clown of the family, and four more sisters, Constance and Hilda, both older than Edith, and Eva and Gwendolyn. Edith, like Grandpapa, was also a convert to Roman Catholicism and this immediately gave the two of them something in common. She was an accomplished horsewoman and a lover of outdoor life and together they spent many an afternoon riding and walking. They soon became constant companions. For Grandpapa the bitter intrigues of his own family life made the friendship of a down-to-earth girl like Edith all the more important. 'I like you', he wrote to her, 'because you are honest and unselfish, because you are the only straightforward person I have ever met.' By the end of 1899 Edith had become his close confidante, for in her he had at last found somebody with whom he could share not only his troubles about his mother but also all his ideas. His brilliantly entertaining letters to her, which continued right through their eventual marriage until his death, covered every imaginable subject from politics to practical jokes. He addressed her as 'Honoured and Well-Beloved Co-Religionist', sometimes abbreviated to HWBCR, and signed himself 'TT', the 'Terrible Turk'.

24/3'4900

Honoured and Well-beloved Co-religionist

Ha! Ha! my sense of humour is excessively tickled

I have just received your third nay fourth farewell letter written doubtless while I was wiring you my leave extension, I beg you will therefore excuse my smiles, again I — really —I am — laughing so I can't WRITE!!

HA Ha! — HO! HO! AH! AH.

please don't! — HA! – HA! — oof! I am exhausted

NOW I'M l-la-ha-ha-fing ag-ha-hain O dear, I shall never be able to write this HA! HA!

HA! HA! let-ha-ha-ter ha! ha! ugh-huh-ugh-le-hah! I just have drunk a glass of water — 0-h-h, now I am recovered and can proceed.

O my dear Co-religionist a 1000 thanks for your letter it's long enough since I have laughed — pray therefore excuse it on paper, barely having recovered exhausted, and with aching sides, I pray you'll excuse a shaking hand,

Well up comes a few in my mind directly my thoughts revert to this old train, will I really believe my troubles are at an end INSHA — LL — AH.

WE ALHAM DO-LIL- OHH, I have every hope the 4days

The year 1900 saw the publication of Grandpapa's first book. Entitled *Through Five Turkish Provinces* it was the account of a journey he had made, while still an undergraduate, along the Euphrates to Baghdad and then north up towards the Russian border. He was accompanied on this trip, as he had been on previous occasions, by Isa Kubrusli, a guide he had known since his childhood travels with Sir Tatton. In the late 1860s Isa had served Lord Chelmsford in the Abyssinian compaign and accompanied Sir Charles Wilson on his expedition to Mount Sinai, but in latter years he found himself working in the Jerusalem office of travel agent Thomas Cook, on hire to English tourists. This was a job he did not particularly enjoy as he found the English of the 1890s a different breed to those he had once known. His views on these people were uttered in broken English which Grandpapa phonetically translated as follows: 'Before time the Henglish very rich; always he have long barbe; always he ride it like really man; shoot it very good; and give plenty baksheesh.' Now, however, 'many very fat and wear rubbish clotheses; many very old men; many very meselable; some ride like monkeys; and some I see afraid from the horses. Den noder kind of Henglish he not believe notin; he laugh for everything and everybody; he call us poor meselable black; he say everything is nonsense and was no God and notin . . .' Grandpapa, whom Isa regarded as one of the old guard, and whom he had taken to calling his 'son', added his own disapproval of the new 'tourists'. 'It is easy to conceive that such a man should imagine that the English have degenerated when he sees the ill-mannered and irreverent mob that now flock to Jerusalem; and I have often wondered if those insensate vulgarians who, to the accompaniment of bells and blaring horns, scorch along the road to Bethlehem, have any idea of the righteous contempt which they earn for themselves and their unfortunate country.'

As well as Isa, Grandpapa's expedition included 'a cook, a waiter, four muleteers and a groom; seven Syrian mules, fine willing beasts capable of carrying heavy loads; two good country horses for myself and one each for the cook and the waiter, a Persian pony for the dragoman; and last, though not least, a Kurdish sheep dog that not only attended the pitching and striking of the camp, but after nightfall undertook the entire responsibility of guarding it'. Being a keen photographer he also carried with him his Kodak camera, although in the preface to the book he apologizes for not having been able to 'give many more illustrations: but my films were "fogged" in the process of development – a result which, I am informed, frequently happens when professionals deal with the work of amateurs'. This was to be the start of a large collection of photographs of all his travels.

In *Through Five Turkish Provinces* Grandpapa gave free rein to his love of underlining the comic and exaggerating the grotesque, of which his description of the approach to Mosul is a perfect example.

The first thing that struck me was a splendid bridge. It is a fine piece of workmanship and has only one fault: it does not cross the river. The engineer commenced building it about 170 yards from the bank: he built piers and at the twenty-fourth came to the water. Then after due consideration he thought that he would build the bridge with boats, and these he chained to the end of the bridge masonry. Though this structure is useless as a bridge, it makes an excellent rendezvous for beggars, lepers and streetmeat vendors.'

The reviews of this book were 'one series of ignorant, meaningless praise' and Grandpapa revealed his scorn for them in a letter to Alfred Dowling. 'I can perfectly imagine how it's done: Editor: "O, look here, a book by that young fellow Sykes! Cut it up. Oh no! he's a son of Tatton Sykes. You remember those trials, he'll be deuced rich!" Result: "Mr Sykes' brilliant little production on his trip to Siberia shows energy, valour and literary talent of no small order." '

Grandpapa and Isa Kubrusli, the guide he had known since childhood.

Grandpapa had hardly had time to finish work on *Through Five Turkish Provinces* before he was called up for active service in South Africa. This could not have come at a worse time as he was trapped in the midst of the most bitter wrangling over the settlement of his mother's debts. If Sir Tatton had had his way he would have been quite happy to wash his hands of Jessica. This was something that Grandpapa could never have allowed to happen, and he was determined to force his father to reach a settlement with him so that together they could rescue her from the final disgrace of complete bankruptcy. Grandpapa was terrified he would have to leave for the war before any settlement was reached, as Sir Tatton kept delaying the proceedings. Grandpapa immediately suspected the worst. 'My father', he wrote to Edith, 'now says he won't do anything before I return from the war because, says he, "I might be killed and then he wouldn't have to pay anything at all"'. This hardly strikes me as a very noble thought.'

It was Edith who was Grandpapa's saviour during this period of appalling pressure, for to her he was able to pour out his innermost feelings. 'Will my worries never end? I begin to doubt it. From all this a surly misanthropy begins to pervade my nature. I hate my kind, I hate, I detest human beings, their deformities, their cheating, their cunning all fill me with savage rage; their filthiness, their stench appals me. I detest the whole human race except some individuals. The stupidity of the wise, the wickedness of the ignorant, but you must forgive, remember I have never had a childhood ...' Their daily correspondence gave him the strength he needed and, on the eve of his departure to South Africa, when a settlement had been finally agreed on, he wrote to her: 'O my dear co-religionist, what a relief, and you in a way have helped to bring this about, you gave me by your last letter courage and good humour enough to last out till the end. Thank God you exist.... You don't know what a blessing you have been to me. I see you in the photograph maliciously saying "If it hadn't been me, it would have been someone else." Well if you'll excuse me saying so, you're a liar!!'

Grandpapa hated his first nine months in South Africa. He found the country infernally dull, there was little for him to do and anyway his thoughts were, as always, elsewhere. 'O for the East, the East and real feelings! There fighting is real fighting, blind healthy rage and fury! Here it is stealth and dodging and nothing else, and so unending.' Things brightened up considerably however in the autumn of 1900 when he was transferred with his company to Rhenoster Bridge, a turning point in his experience of the Boer War, for at last he was to feel he was doing something of importance. It was here that he experienced his first taste of action, writing to Alfred Dowling, in a fit of excitement, 'to inform you that I, Mark Sykes, have been under fire, not in a very heavy one, but still I have been actually within sight and touch of the Boers.' Now that he really felt part of the war, soldiering began to get under his skin. He took a particular interest in field fortifications. 'I was mentioned in despatches for work done in field fortifications and for this again I have to thank the library at Sledmere. When I was a little boy I made myself familiar with the fieldwork manuals of the eighteenth century, and when the Boers had lost all their artillery eighteenth-century fieldworks were the very thing – out of date against a modern army with artillery, but perfectly sound against ordinary rifle fire. I adopted in the Boer War most of the hints I had picked up from Marshal Saxe's *Art of War 1740*.'

Within a short time of his arrival Grandpapa refined the defences of Rhenoster Bridge to a point where he felt that the 100 men there could hold out against 600 of the enemy. Rhenoster Bridge, said the chief engineer, was the best on the line. One of his devices was a trench system constructed at certain points along the railway, its purpose being to secure the line and save lives. The work had been carried out, at

The part of his Boer War experience which interested Grandpapa most was the construction of field fortifications, for which he used Kaffir workmen, of whom he had a high opinion.

174

Grandpapa was upset by the army's treatment of blacks, who, during the summer of 1901, were being used as night-watchmen.
Though supposed to be volunteers the men had in fact been pressed into duty, armed only with old Martini rifles
and twenty rounds of ammunition. The British soldiers were never allowed out of camp with less than fifty rounds.
Furthermore, a captured British soldier had the option of surrender whereas a black would be flogged and shot. Witnessing
this flogging in 1901, he commented, 'The man received 33 lashes from a heavy hide whip. He made no sign of pain.'

his own instigation but against army regulations, by black Kaffir workmen, of whom he had a high opinion. 'They cheer me every morning and volunteer to work for me. I give them a good pinch of snuff every other evening, and watch them while they work. They are different to Arabs as they continually roar with laughter.' Though Grandpapa tried hard to draw the attention of his superiors to the merits of using native labour to build fortifications rather than waste soldiers, he had little success, getting only jeers and jokes for his efforts. He was more than a little shocked by the total disregard they seemed to have for either the abilities or the lives of the blacks. Those lucky enough to be under his command fared a great deal better than most of their comrades, in the matter of diet, for example: 'How like our nincompoops to feed them on salt beef, one pound per day, and biscuit, one pound per day, men who never touch meat, and whose fare from their infancy has been mealie pap and sugar. However I have put that piece of folly straight.'

176

'The gun is a great success as far as I can see. One of the scornful today came up and said, 'Haw-whe-ahs this blessed invisible jim-jam of yours eh?' I said, 'Within four hundred yards of you in the open, look for it!' (My temper was getting rather short.) The fool then said, 'It's an awfly clever trick don't you know, but of course it's quite impractical. How could they march past if no-one could see the guns? Haw, haw, haw!'

(From a letter to Edith)

When Grandpapa returned from South Africa he found the village decorated with triumphal arches.
(opposite) Grandpapa standing on the steps of Sledmere shortly after his return.

It was the spring of 1902 before Grandpapa found himself back home again, now as Captain Sykes and sporting a moustache. His return gave Sledmere an excellent excuse to make up for not having been able to celebrate his coming of age in 1900. Arriving at Fimber station by car (the railway line having been blocked by a derailment) he was greeted by members of the 2nd East Yorkshire Battalion and band, along with leading figures of the estate, under a huge 'Welcome Home' banner. It was pouring with rain. There was a brief welcoming speech, and then a three-mile procession to Sledmere with Grandpapa riding in an open carriage. The main village street was spanned by a huge arch trimmed with horseshoes bearing the words 'Good Luck', while a second proclaimed 'Honour The Brave'. From every building hung bunting, flowers and evergreen boughs, while the pavements were lined with children waving Union Jacks. Outside the gates of the house stood a raised platform beneath another arch welcoming him home. Here one of the oldest tenants presented Sledmere's hero with an illuminated address congratulating him on his service to the country. The following day a large dinner and ball were held in two elaborately decorated marquees which had been set up in the park.

When, to his great relief, the fuss over his return was finally over, Grandpapa found himself once again under various pressures. First of all there was the old spectre of his mother whom he found at 2 Chesterfield Street 'in a terrible state'. She had obviously got hopelessly drunk out of nervousness at seeing her son for the first time in three years. This upset Grandpapa dreadfully. 'O dearest co-relig,' he confided to Edith, 'forgive me if I trouble you with private griefs, but you are my only friend . . . . I must admit that things are worse in every way than they were two years ago. I was only talking to you the other day about being without a home . . . . If ever I seem to you undemonstrative pray remember my past and

181

present life and, remembering that, forgive my shortcomings.' Had it not been for Edith, who urged him to be patient, there might have been an irreparable breach with Jessica during this period for which Grandpapa would have never forgiven himself.

Another pressure under which he found himself came from quite a different direction. This was to go into politics as a Conservative for the local constituency of Buckrose. Though his experiences in the Boer War had given Grandpapa a taste for responsibility, he didn't yet feel ready to enter the world of Parliament, a world for which he had a healthy contempt, and the Conservatives of Buckrose had no luck. 'I have told them that I am neither a buffoon, an office-seeker nor a hypocrite, that I cannot talk sonorous twaddle for endless hours, that I have neither a large stomach nor a white waistcoat, that I have no sympathy with the opposition, but I consider the present government the most hopeless incompetent jelly that has ever quivered in a British Cabinet. With which I left them and bade adieu to the Conservatives of East Yorkshire.'

Grandpapa kept these pressures at bay by immersing himself in plans for a journey to the East which he had dreamed about while in South Africa. This he undertook in October along with a Cambridge friend, John Hugh Smith or 'Little John', whose character he thought would be well rounded off by a strong dose of rough travel. As Isa Kubrusli had died while he was in South Africa Grandpapa found himself a new guide whom he called Jacobal Arab. He felt it was glorious to be back in the East and much enjoyed playing the part of cicerone to Little John, eagerly introducing him to all the excitements of these strange lands. 'He wants to try hashish and says it will be a new emotion. I think I shall let him, particularly as the soda-water is not of the same excellent and hot-copper-cooling brand as at Cambridge. It will cure him of any other dangerous investigations he may wish to perpetrate. O ye hammering anvils! O ye clanging smithies! O ye piercing broad-awls! O ye throbbing tom-toms! What a headache he will get!'

The journey took them from Beirut to Aleppo where they split up, taking different routes to Urfa, Grandpapa taking the most rugged route through the Taurus Mountains, and Little John the easier one through the valley of the Euphrates. From Urfa they travelled east to Diarbekr where once again they parted ways, Little John taking a raft down the Tigris to collect stores in Baghdad. They reunited at Kerkuk and set off towards the Russian border, after which point they were plagued with disaster. At Sulymaniyah both fell ill. At Kevi Sanjak Little John had a fight with Jacobal Arab who threatened to stab him in revenge. In the Kurdish mountains they were twice misdirected by uncooperative Kurds, and Grandpapa's fine Arab stallion collapsed and died from strain. The remainder of the journey to the Russian border, Tiflis and Batum was merely a repetition of Grandpapa's trip as an undergraduate, Little John having stubbornly refused to take the different route Grandpapa had planned. It was this kind of disagreement that in the end made Grandpapa wish he had travelled alone.

Awaiting her 'Terrible Turk' in Constantinople was Edith, who had followed every inch of the journey in his letters to her. On their return to England they decided that the time was right for them to get married, something they had both had in their minds for a long time. Their only anxiety was how Sir Tatton would react to the news. To their delight he was most enthusiastic, stipulating only that the wedding should take place in York, which they happily agreed. They were married on 28 October 1903 in St Wilfred's, York, with Henry Cholmondeley as best man, and their honeymoon took them from Paris and Rome to Constantinople and Jerusalem. It was a marriage destined to be a rapturous success.

Grandpapa and his friend John Hugh Smith, 'Little John', for whom he had prescribed a dose of rough travel, before their journey together through the Ottoman Empire and part of Russia in 1902.

183

'*About half an hour after leaving Erkenek we breasted a rise against the skyline, Jacob leading; when he reached the top I heard him cry, "Allah-Ham-do-lillah! Allah Hamdolillah!" and throwing his cap in the air he jumped down from his horse. In a moment I joined him, and saw to my delight an immense stretch of snowless green wooded*

valley and hills; the thaw had cleared all, and from miserable, bitter, icy winter we descended in ten minutes into pleasant, balmy, early spring. Birds were singing in the trees, the clouds rolled back, and we thanked our God we were delivered from the most awful journey I have ever undertaken.'

(Extract from Dar Ul Islam, 1904)

Grandpapa now tasted the fruits of his first literary success. On his return from South Africa he had got together with Edmond Sandars, another old Cambridge friend, and while at Sledmere they had read the latest books on military science, such as the *Infantry Drill Book* of 1896 and a *Handbook on Field Artillery* by a Lieutenant-Colonel Pratt. They then wrote a parody of these very serious works called *Tactics and Military Training* by 'Major-General George D'Ordel', which in binding and format was an exact replica of the *Infantry Drill Book*. The book was dedicated to another old War Office hand, 'General Sir John Barbecue K.C.B.' who, like D'Ordel, had learned 'modern warfare' in the Crimea, ignored the South African War on the grounds of its 'irregular conduct', and disapproved of 'the new craze for learning and innovation'. *Tactics* was published posthumously as D'Ordel himself had died in his chair at the United Military and Naval Club after reading the new drill book by Lord Roberts, a serious army reformer. It was opened at the preface, and a deep nail mark underscored the following passage: 'Nor are the men allowed to degenerate into mere machines. The efficiency of the individual as a fighting man is the test of a good batallion.' The book was a considerable success, going through six editions in the space of a few weeks, and creating widespread attention in all London's daily papers and weekly reviews. At the same time it gained great popularity in military circles by managing to make a serious point about army reform in an amusing but incisive way.

The success of the book was something that Grandpapa had not anticipated, and it brought his name to the lips of many people as one of the brightest young men around, with the possibility of a brilliant future ahead of him. One of these people happened to be the dashing Conservative, George Wyndham, Chief Secretary of Ireland, who offered him a post as his private secretary. Edith was ambitious for Grandpapa, seeing his potential as a politician and, in spite of his own uncertainty, she persuaded him to accept; she knew there could be few better stepping-stones into political life. He left for Dublin immediately after his honeymoon, but without Edith as the summons was at such short notice, and to begin with things did not go too well. He disliked the apparent slackness of Dublin. There was no sign of George Wyndham when he arrived, nor anybody to show him the ropes. This irked him after the efficient regime he had become used to in South Africa, and he was almost ready to quit before he had started. 'Give me a native regiment to organize, a rebellion to raise, a map to make, a blockhouse line to construct, a village to govern and I will do it. Give me an independent command, anything you choose but this – the life of a cat . . . .'

As it turned out Grandpapa's Irish career was a short one in which he was continually frustrated by not being given enough to do by Wyndham. He never wasted a single moment of his time, however, for he used this period of inactivity to pursue further his literary career. He began by completing *Dar-ul-Islam*, a book based on his journey with Little John the previous year. The theme that ran through the book was his intense dislike of Western intrusion in the traditions of the East, a theme that appealed to H. G. Wells who wrote to him, 'I like your "down" on civilization and such like.' It was the start of a lasting friendship between them. Rudyard Kipling said that he had been unable to go to bed until he had finished the book and that it had enabled him to see and smell the Ottoman Empire as never before. Praise indeed for a very young author!

His next work was a further d'Ordel collaboration with Edmond Sandars. This time the author was 'Prometheus D'Ordel', cousin of the late Major-General, and its full title was *D'Ordel's Pantechnicon, An Universal Directory of the Mechanical Art of Manufacturing Illustrated Magazines, Intended as a Course of Learning for Future Writers, Containing an Account of the Advance of Literature in Modern Times with a Perfect Model for the Guidance of Students and Directions Exposing the Whole Manual Art of the Trade*. The 'Model Magazine' was called *Scragford's Farthing*, and was an obvious lampoon of publications like the *Strand Magazine*. Included inside, for example, was the obligatory serial novel, *The Search for the Iron Toe*,

"A THING, LIVING, SUFFERING . . WAS FLAYING ITSELF ALIVE BEFORE MY VERY EYES."

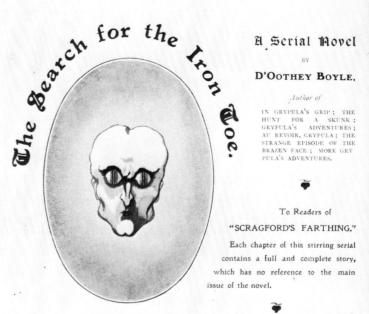

The Search for the Iron Toe.

A Serial Novel

BY

D'OOTHEY BOYLE.

Author of

IN GRYPULA'S GRIP; THE
HUNT FOR A SKUNK;
GRYPULA'S ADVENTURES;
AU REVOIR, GRYPULA; THE
STRANGE EPISODE OF THE
BRAZEN FACE; MORE GRY
PULA'S ADVENTURES.

To Readers of
"SCRAGFORD'S FARTHING."

Each chapter of this stirring serial
contains a full and complete story,
which has no reference to the main
issue of the novel.

Synopsis.

Grypula, cruel, stern, affectionate, repulsive, faithful, fascinating and unscrupulous man of mystery, aged 2003, accompanied by his grey stoat " Moloch," which he carries about in a diamond-studded reticule, has employed Ralf Bunyan, a struggling young Australian chiropodist, as his amanuensis. The latter met his employer in the lions' cage at Jamrach's, and has since been commissioned by his master to record some sixteen hundred of his unique exploits. Ethel Liffey is the niece and sole heiress of the Duke of Dublin, a millionaire noble in Grypula's pay. Ralf has been ordered by his master to keep in touch with the Duke, and contrives to obtain professional employment in the house. · Ethel knows the secret of the Den. Grypula knows everything. Ralf knows nothing.

CHAPTER CLXXVII.

The Adventure of the Missing Lynx.

ON returning home after a pleasant day spent at "Clubland," I found on my table in my brown study a heavily-sealed envelope, which I hastily tore open. It read as follows:

MY BOY,—Ethel and I are lonely to-night; will you partake of supper with us? Your friend—Dublin, Dux K.S.D.

To change my tie and shirt-front and slip into my black velvet Norfolk jacket was the work of a moment, for I knew that his Grace's table, at his mansion in Harley Street, would be well spread. Besides, there was Ethel—but of her more anon. Within a quarter of an hour I applied my thumb to the electric "sonnerie" marked "Visitors," and thought to myself how strange it was that I, the erstwhile struggling young surgical operator, should, through my casual meeting with the most extraordinary of men, now be a welcome guest at one of England's noblest houses. The door opened, and emitted a flood of light on to the pavement, and I was relieved of my top-hat by Buljer the butler,

'D'Ordel's Pantechnicon', published in the summer of 1904, brilliantly lampooned magazines such as the Strand Magazine and appearing as it did after 'D'Ordel's Tactics', well and truly established Grandpapa's reputation as a humourist.

parodying the then popular serials of Conan Doyle. This time the author was 'Doothey Boyle', whose previous masterpieces had included *In Grypula's Grip, Grypula's Adventures, Au Revoir Grypula, The Strange Episode of the Brazen Face,* and *More Grypula's Adventures.* Though one reviewer described the book as 'probably some of the most brilliant nonsense ever written', it did not have the same degree of success as *Tactics,* and the plans for a series of D'Ordel books covering politics, law, etc. were shelved.

So we find Grandpapa at the age of twenty-four with two books, the D'Ordel satires and many travel articles in print, and apparently well on the way to becoming an author of some stature, a profession in which his perceptiveness, imagination and wit would have stood him in good stead. Yet literary success seemed to hold little meaning for him and his ambition remained unfulfilled by writing. He still felt deep down that his destiny lay in the Ottoman Empire where he longed to have a post of importance. 'I am thinking', he wrote to Edith, 'of asking Wyndham for a job, either in India under G. Nathanial Curzon, or on the reorganization of the militia. I prefer the first, if you do, but await your word. I must have an employment which I am capable of working in – that is to say one requiring energy, thought and originality.'

In September 1904 Edith gave birth to their first child, a girl whom they named Freya. Soon afterwards Grandpapa was given a post as an honorary attaché in the British embassy in Constantinople, not quite what he had had in mind, but at least it would take him to the East. By the time he and Edith were settled in Turkey in the early summer of 1905, Edith was once again heavily pregnant. This time the baby was a son and heir for Sledmere. They called him Richard, much to the delight of Jessica who considered it a good family name, 'much better than Tatton!'

To begin with Grandpapa was delighted with his new job, writing home to Henry Cholmondeley, 'I am now very satisfied with my work which is much more real than the Irish Office.' But his enthusiasm was short-lived, for the old frustrations soon set in. Because of Grandpapa's previous travels and great ambitions he did not really fit into the pattern of most honorary attachés who were there merely for a prolonged postgraduate Grand Tour in the East before settling down. He had hoped that he would have more influence with the ambassador, rather than spending his days doing worthless tasks like pasting in press cuttings. Grandpapa believed that it was of vital importance for Britain to keep up the good relationship with Turkey which was formed in the nineteenth century, when Russia was a common enemy to them both, and that she should guard against British predominance there being undermined by the Germans who were building railways and helping to train the Turkish army. So, instead of sitting back, he wrote reports on his journeys around the province and used them as a vehicle for his views. They fell on deaf ears. He was, after all, only an honorary attaché, even if he did have an inflated ego. As far as Whitehall was concerned, though his reports with their maps and photographs may have made entertaining reading, they lacked the form and objectivity to be taken seriously.

Grandpapa now began to realize that, however great a part of his life he may have spent travelling in the East, and however much he might feel that it was his place, it made little difference to his prospects of influencing government policy towards that part of the world. He became increasingly aware that things were controlled from London, and for this reason he began to consider Parliament as a serious proposition, writing to Edith, 'When I see this country and think of our lost opportunities, it makes me mad .... Are we a declining nation? Are we falling into the hands of hidebound official clauses and settling everything by competitive exam? . . . Politics will be great fun in a year's time, O don't you ever fear, I'm going into them. We will give battle to cant and incompetence.'

Grandpapa, Edith, Freya and Richard, 1906.

With this plan firmly in mind, he despatched Edith and the children home to England in March 1906 so that she could get them settled in time for his return. He himself set off by horse on one last great journey across to Sinope on the Black Sea where Edith met him for the last leg of the trip. By this time they had been separated for four months and he was pining for her: 'I don't know', he wrote on hearing of her imminent arrival, 'how I shall pass the next three weeks without you my dearest, but it will be like heaven when you come.' Together they rode a thousand miles, from Sinope east across to the Persian border, then west via Aleppo to the Mediterranean where they embarked for London. Grandpapa included an account of this journey in his final major work, *The Caliphs' Last Heritage*, a study of Islam and the Ottoman Empire which he had started to pass the time while at the embassy in Constantinople, and which was not to be published until 1915 when the war in Europe had spread to Turkey and interest in the subject suddenly revived.

In April 1907 Grandpapa was adopted as the Conservative candidate for Buckrose. He saw himself as a Tory Democrat, and he longed for a return to the great days of Disraeli when ideals were to the fore: ideals like that of unity, 'between employer and employed, class and class, creed and creed, father and son, colony and motherland, prince and subject, farm and village, village and city, city and kingdom, kingdom and colony, colony and empire'. He distrusted the Labour movement as he considered it too rooted in urban bureaucracy and he urged his father-in-law, Sir John Gorst, 'to drive in the idea that a good landlord is much cheaper than a corrupt, pushing, clique-ridden, middleclass, salary-cadging bureaucracy, which seems to me to be what the solicitor's clerk who calls himself a "Labour member" desires'. But he never underestimated the power of the movement. 'If I were a working man, my house insanitary, my wages low, my child sweated, my wife ailing, my employment hazardous, I should vote labour.' He called for landlords who neglected their estates to be broken like reeds and for every Tory member to show himself at heart a true Labour member. The Tories must outdo the trade unionists in getting the working man 'a good house, a good wage, a good education', with employers having to assume more responsibility towards their employees. The congestion of cities should be relieved by moving more people into the countryside, and great landowners encouraged by the government to build cottages for slum-dwellers, while the suburbs should no longer be limited to the 'stockholder and the solicitor', but should also offer a haven to 'the rivetter, the navvy and the stevedore'.

That Grandpapa was extremely conscientious as a candidate is shown by the great volume and variety of his correspondence during this period. He took great pains to answer all the letters and requests of local people, however humble. A good example of this is to be found in a letter he wrote to a Mr Turner, a shoemaker from Beverley, who had evidently written to say that he felt in need of a wider education and asked Grandpapa's advice. In his reply Grandpapa laid out a list of what he considered to be essential reading, ranging from the Book of Ecclesiastes to the novels of Disraeli, as well as a detailed programme as to how they should be approached. At the end of the letter, which covered several pages, he added: 'I shall be glad to help you in any way while you go through this period of study and, if you wish it, note your essays etc. or criticize them.'

Unfortunately for Grandpapa local issues at this time were very much overshadowed by more important national issues, such as the famous Lloyd George budget of 1910 which was blocked by the House of Lords. This aroused class feeling all over the country and in Buckrose the Liberals made capital out of the difference between their member Sir Luke White, a self-made man, and his aristocratic opponent Mark. 'Follow the Gospel, and put Mark before Luke', cried the Sykes supporters, but all to no avail. Sir Luke White had been a popular M.P. since 1905 and, despite Grandpapa's hard campaigning, was returned in both elections of 1910. It must be said that Grandpapa did not help himself in the second of these by publicly referring to his opponent in a moment of temper as 'an old humbug', out of which Sir

In 1906 Edith joined Grandpapa at Sinope on the Black Sea,
and together they rode back across to the Mediterranean, a journey of a thousand miles.

Luke made suitable capital. He appeared at all Liberal meetings, but instead of speaking he enacted a semi-dumb show. He endeavoured to speak, found himself overcome by emotion, and with the tears streaming down his cheeks could only repeat the words, 'E ca'd me a Oomboog'. He won the election all right. Grandpapa was philosophical about these defeats: 'If you choose to give me a political career', he said, 'I will take it up, but if not, I have my books and can go back to my plough.'

In the years between 1897 and 1906 Grandpapa had spent more months abroad than in England. From 1907 to 1911 he was to spend more time at home with his family than he ever would again. With Sir Tatton still reigning supreme at Sledmere Grandpapa leased from him a 400-acre farm on the estate called Eddlethorpe, which he immediately set about altering and enlarging to his own liking, assisted by the estate architect Mr Collett. When Sir Tatton agreed to pay for the alterations he can have had no idea what Grandpapa had in mind, for when he and Mr Collett were finished Eddlethorpe was changed

Eddlethorpe, the farm on the estate which Grandpapa altered and enlarged to his own liking.

beyond recognition. What had once been a plain, two-storey farmhouse had become a flamboyant hotchpotch of designs. There were two new wings, fifteen bedrooms, 'Mark's Tower', a three-storey structure containing his study, library and dressing-room, as well as a chapel, nursery and kitchen approached by four tiled archways, over each of which were Cufic inscriptions. The ground floor exterior was red brick, the stucco upper floors were painted grey, the roof was red, the chimneys white, while the cupola on top of Mark's Tower matched the black and white of the house windows. It was a suitably eccentric building that appealed to Grandpapa's extrovert nature.

Grandpapa's Humber car at Menethorpe where the family lived while Eddlethorpe was being prepared.
(opposite) Edith, with Freya, Richard, Everilda and Christopher.

While all this construction was going on the family lived at another estate farmhouse called Menethorpe, and it was here in November 1907 that Edith gave birth to twins, Everilda and Christopher. When the four children and two adults finally moved into Eddlethorpe, along with numerous servants – a governess for Freya, nurses for Richard and the twins, a butler, footman, cook and chauffeur – its empty rooms filled with life, and its increased size came into its own. With his own family Grandpapa now found that he could make up for things he had missed as an only child. He was able to indulge all his fantasies. He had, for example, a passion for trains, and within no time an elaborate clockwork railway system was winding its way around the top passages. My Aunt Freya remembers well how seriously he used to take the trains, and how he once flew at her because she caused a derailment.

Just as his mother had done with him, so Grandpapa treated children as small members of the adult world, as is shown by an incident recalled by Great Uncle Harold Gorst, Edith's brother. Richard, aged two, was having a tantrum, lying on his back, kicking at all who came near, and screaming his refusal to go for his usual walk with the nurse. When Grandpapa arrived on the scene both the nurse and Edith were at their wits' end.

Suddenly Mark, after surveying his son and heir with that queer little contraction of his eyebrows, swooped down, picked him up in his arms, bore him away kicking and struggling into a neighbouring bedroom and locked the door behind him. We stood there with blanched faces, expecting at any minute to hear the sounds of a hearty spanking. But the shouts of the youthful Richard died down with extraordinary rapidity and complete silence followed. In three or four minutes Mark came out of the room leading a perfectly serene and normal Richard by the hand. With a pleasant and rather superior smile he handed him over to the nurse. 'What did you do to effect such a miracle?', I asked Mark later. 'I sat him in a dry basin on the washstand', he said, 'and reasoned with him.'

That was Grandpapa's philosophy in a nutshell.

After his second election defeat in 1910, George Wyndham wrote to Grandpapa urging him not to take the defeat to heart and promising him, 'I shall insist on your being offered a good seat . . . and when I say insist I mean that I am going to take my gloves off.' But Grandpapa could not help feeling discouraged and he decided that if he were to recover his spirits sufficiently to enter another election campaign, he should get out of the country by himself for a while. This he did, and from North Africa and Algeria, which he loathed, he travelled to Spain where he fell in love with the art and architecture. His description in a letter to Edith of the church in Piedra Buena is a masterpiece of observation:

Take King's College chapel, block up all the windows in 1620, put up altars every six years from 1720 to 1845, paint all the stalls green in 1850, and yellow and red in 1870, but never scrape off the colours; paint the groining pink and the background pale blue with gold stars; open one of the blocked windows in 1848 and fill with English stained glass; hang pictures of hell and the martyrdom of St Lawrence on the walls beyond the reach of a duster; move the choir to the back of the church in 1730, block up the main door, knock a hole in the chancel and make that the door; lay a statue in a winding sheet, with half-closed glass eyes that roll, full length on one of the altars (in the dark it looks like a real corpse); light a little red lamp under a life-size crucifix with real hair and blood varnished to shine in the flickering of the lamp; put a statue of Our Lady in black *crêpe* and silk, with crinoline, gum tears on cheeks, glass eyes, real hair, covered with gold, silver, brass and tinsel, in a glass case and cut a squint in the wall so that the light shines horribly on a white face in a dark cell; fill every spare corner with candlesticks, vases, lecterns, benches, clear away all chairs and put down rush mats, and you have an average Spanish Gothic church.

When Grandpapa returned to England, relaxed and revived, his political chance finally came when he was adopted by and won the constituency of Central Hull. He was chosen because, after Buckrose, he was well known in the area, as was his mother who was well loved for her work among the poor in Hull. Edith was a great help to him in his campaign, having always encouraged him and been interested herself

As a speaker Grandpapa was brilliant and unorthodox, though there were often a few awkward moments before he got into his stride. (opposite) Grandpapa's election poster when he stood as candidate for Hull.

in politics, and she served as his political confidante. In a letter telling her how he had felt on his first day in the House, he wrote: 'I found a nice old thing with a top hat who looks after coats and who said, "I have seen two generations and you're the third – Mr George Bentinck, Mr Christopher and yourself," though he made it clear that he felt the standard of speeches left a lot to be desired . . . . The speeches are enough to drive one mad with boredom – "While entirely agreeing-er-with the first remarks-er-of my right honourable-er-friend-I-er-hem-depreciate-er-deprecate – that is I am in agreement with a part – that is the first, the first part . . ." etc. These men cannot deliver themselves of their ideas.'

As a speaker himself Grandpapa, once he got started, was always eloquent and anything but boring, though there were always a few awkward moments before he got into his stride.

He would get up, slide his hands down the sides of his trousers, push back a lock of hair that always fell over his forehead, and jerk out a few disjointed phrases in a halting tone of voice: 'Mr Speaker . . . well I think . . . that is to say, well . . . some honourable member . . . perhaps!' Then off he would go without a single pause, using picturesque and expressive language, making his points clearly and impressively, and always fascinating his audience by the humorous way in which he viewed the subject under discussion. He had a faint smile on his face when he was making an amusing point which seemed to beseech his audience to see things in the same humorous light. His eyes twinkled, and he had a way of contracting his eyebrows which gave him a very quizzical look.

His maiden speech in the House, on the subject of the Turko–Italian War, was an outstanding success. He deliberately chose a foreign affairs debate as it enabled him to make use of his unique experience of the Near East and, as luck would have it, he happened to speak before the Prime Minister. Following the tradition that a maiden speaker is always congratulated by the member speaking after him, Mr Asquith praised the Tory recruit for 'as promising and successful a maiden speech as almost any I have listened to in my experience'. In a letter to Lady Londonderry the following day, Grandpapa put it all down to 'an extraordinary run of luck: (a) Dillon had wearied the House till it was ready to cheer anyone on anything; (b) I knew the subject; (c) it was not controversial; (d) Asquith himself is a Yorkshire man. Take also into consideration that it was a pure fluke that the P.M. spoke directly after me.'

Grandpapa's new job suited him down to the ground. Not only was he involved in an activity which he felt was worthy of himself and the traditions of his ancestors, but it was a life that was perfectly suited to his restless temperament and active mind. For once there was more than enough for him to do, with all the business in the House, as well as endless trips to and from his constituency, a fact which meant that he was almost always in a frantic hurry to meet his schedule. One day, for example, Great Uncle Harold, who was staying with him, was lingering over a delicious cup of coffee before tucking into his breakfast, when into the dining-room rushed Grandpapa, shouting that the car was waiting and they must leave at once. Poor Great Uncle Harold, who really had no idea what Grandpapa was talking about, protested that he was just sitting down to his breakfast. ' "Breakfast!", shouted Mark, much incensed at the delay, "Here's breakfast, I'll take it with me!" He rushed to the table and, seizing several pieces of bacon on toast, thrust them into his overcoat pocket. A couple of grilled sausages and a slice of ham with plenty of fat on it followed. Into another pocket he stuffed the top off a loaf of bread. Then he seized me also . . . and rushed me out of the room into the hall.'

I do not intend to go into Grandpapa's political career in detail as it is admirably covered elsewhere, and I am more concerned with his general character. There are, however, two points worth making. The first is that throughout his career he maintained a refreshingly naïve belief that, whatever the incompatibilities between adherents of the Christian faith, between left and right wings, Irish

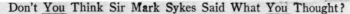

Don't You Think Sir Mark Sykes Said What You Thought?

DAILY SKETCH.

No. 1,581.   LONDON, FRIDAY, APRIL 3, 1914.   [Registered as a Newspaper.]   ONE HALFPENNY.

THE GENESIS OF A GREAT SPEECH: THE NOTES FROM WHICH SIR MARK SYKES, "M.P. FOR ENGLAND," SAID WHAT ALL SANE MEN ARE THINKING.

Sir Mark Sykes electioneering.

PERS: DISTRESS: G.W.: ARM: IRE: COMP: DISAST
BLAME: BOTH: PASS PRANK. CLASS. CREED. NAT
=MIL: FORCES: & QUARRELS:
PAUSE: TO-DAY FUT YAWNS: ABYSS: Q SETTLED
NOTHING SAVE C: DISINTEG
WHO WINS: RUIN: RAD=CO ULST CON 30Y
=IRE BLOODSHED =ARMY: COM DIS: RICH: POOR:
=SUSP DELA = NAVY = H.C. FAC = LAB: TROUBS
=INDIA LOYAL. ANARCH. FAN: FOR POS HOPE
PERS: 1895: ADMIT IMPOS: NEW FORCES
LAB: EMP: I.Q. FUND G.W.
R.H.G. FA. QUOTE: AGREE. BASIS?
6.Y PIOUS HOPE: WAY OUT:
= BOTH PARTIES UNDERTKING GIVE. COUNT CONS
A=IMP LOCAL FAC B: LOC: BIZ=CENT PARTY HAG
EARNEST: LIB XCLUDE ULST UNTIL FED
      : CONS ACCEPT H.R. COMPAT FED
SET=FUT: BRIGHT: EV CLASS. SOC. REF. ADMIN.
DEF: SQUIRE: LAB: LEADER ALL NECESS EMP.
IMPOS: POL: MIRE. RAGE. HATE. PETTINESS.
+SMALLEST: GREATEST MERITS.
..APPEAL. IRISH: UN: NAT HELP.

Sir Mark's ingenious "notes" for his great speech.

Sir Mark at a pageant

Sir Mark as a soldier.

It is impossible to say who is to blame. If one sitting on the Back Benches may dare to say so, I feel that the blame must lie upon all. We have drifted on passions, and both sides have gone from one wild cry to another, until we have divided class from class, creed from creed, in order to further our policies, until at the very end of it all one cannot deny that the military forces, and even the very Throne itself, has been involved in our quarrels.

Sir Mark in private life.

What Sir Mark Sykes, the Yorkshire M.P., said in the House of Commons, where they are still discussing the Home Rule Bill, is what all sane men in England think to-day, though Party politicians last night still tried to inflame the old spirit. "I have never experienced so great a feeling of personal distress as during the last nine days," he said, "and blame, to a certain extent, must rest on all. . . . Mark unconsciously altered it as he went along.

How the second paragraph in the above "notes" was elaborated in the House of Commons. (The future yawns before us in a terrible way. Unless this question of Irish government is settled now nothing can save the country and the Empire from ultimate disintegration. . . . Whichever Party won there would be bloodshed in Ireland. Above are the "notes" prepared by Sir Mark for his great speech, and the official report from "Hansard," showing how, in making the speech, Sir

Grandpapa's speech in the Home Rule debate of 1914 earned him the title of 'M.P. for England'.
(opposite) As a budding young politician Grandpapa spent many weekends as a guest in Tory country houses.
In this photograph taken at Hackwood the people are (left to right) Lady Curzon, Marquis Curzon of Keddlestone,
Mrs Winston Churchill, Mr Winston Churchill, Lord D'Abernan, Lady Salisbury, Lady D'Abernan and Sir Mark Sykes.

Nationalists and Unionists, Great Britain and France, Arabs and Zionists, it was always possible to smooth over such conflicts by persuading the parties involved to behave tolerantly and reasonably towards each other. It was this basic philosophy that prompted him to reason with Richard in the wash basin and which, over the Irish Question in 1914, earned for him the title 'M.P. for England'. Secondly, it is remarkable how much he managed to cram on to his plate, for he had many other interests outside politics to which he devoted a considerable amount of time. These included the army, in particular the territorials and his own invention the Waggoners Reserve, the planning and execution of military spectaculars for the Royal Tournament, and the massive task of rebuilding Sledmere House.

One of Grandpapa's favourite annual pastimes was helping in the planning of the Royal Naval and Military Tournaments
in which his 5th Yorkshire Regiment used to take part. Here he had full scope to put to use his knowledge of military strategy.
(opposite) Each year a farm-wagon driving competition was held on the Sledmere estate, and prizes were awarded for the best driving,
quickest harnessing, etc. It was during one of these competitions that Grandpapa realized the potential of these men
in time of war as field-battery drivers. With this in mind he formed a regiment of waggoners which he called 'The Waggoners Reserve'.
In 1914, in one of his most ambitious competitions, 200 drivers put their horses and green-painted waggons through exacting routines.
(overleaf) The work-force employed on the rebuilding of Sledmere.
The house was rebuilt exactly as it was before in the space of four years, at a cost of £43,000.

It was the outbreak of the First World War that presented Grandpapa with his greatest political opportunity, for it allowed him scope to use all his knowledge and experience of the Middle East in helping to shape British policy towards that part of the world. This meant that he spent the greater part of the war on special missions to the East, a fact which, when it ended, gave rise to accusations of 'shirking' and cowardice from his political opponents. Lloyd George was quick to defend him, testifying that he had had 'frequent opportunities of seeing the result of Sir Mark's work, which was of an exceptionally arduous and difficult character, both at home and abroad on special missions to the eastern fronts'. The charges were 'unfounded' and 'cruel'. Edith added her own defence: 'No one can say he has been a shirker. He has been working very hard since the war began. In fact he has hardly ever had a day to go home, and has hardly seen anything of the children. I know there is no man in England who works harder than he does or works longer hours.' The electorate were convinced of Grandpapa's innocence and they returned him to Central Hull, in the 1918 general election, with a majority of over 10,000.

But the arduous work and long hours that Edith had spoken of had taken their toll of Grandpapa, slowly sapping his strength, and when she saw him in Paris at the end of January 1919, where he was awaiting the peace conference, she was so appalled by his appearance that she begged him to go home and rest. He did not follow her advice. A week later Edith fell victim to the devastating epidemic of influenza that was then sweeping Europe, and was confined to her bed in the Hotel Lotti. But while she recovered, Grandpapa was not so lucky. The evening of 10 February he spent with his old D'Ordel collaborator, Edmond Sandars: 'That evening we went to the Opera. As usual Mark acted the music facially and we laughed over the play. He and I went out to smoke in the intervals. He remarked two or three times how much that was good in Paris was due to Napoleon III, in art, building and organization. Sir Arthur Hirtzel drove us all to the Lotti, where Mark left us. After that night he never got out of bed again.'

When Grandpapa died, at 6.30 p.m. on Sunday 13 February, a genuine cry of grief ascended from strange places. English Catholics mourned him in Westminster Cathedral; Jews in Morocco heard his panegyric from the lips of their chief rabbi; in Aleppo and Jerusalem his solemn requiem was sung. On 16 March he would have been forty. 'So', wrote Lord Howard de Walden, 'the one man that I had met who seemed to me to have in him the seeds of greatness was not to attain it after all.' The funeral was held in the private chapel at Sledmere, attended by family and close friends, and afterwards all the inhabitants of the village and many members of the 5th Yorkshire Regiment joined a procession led by the abbot and monks of Ampleforth to Sledmere churchyard for the burial. The flag-draped coffin was borne on a gun-carriage, which was followed by Grandpapa's charger, Punch, bearing an empty saddle and field boots reversed in the stirrups. The regimental band played Chopin's *Marche Funèbre*. A local reporter takes up the scene: 'The father abbot pronounces the commital service, and the body of Sir Mark is in its last resting place, close to that of his father and mother. The firing party fire three rounds into the northern sky, and after each the drums roll and the air seems to tremble with their sadness. Then bayonets are fixed and buglers sound the last post. The widowed mother and fatherless boys fall on their knees, and the hearts of the multitude are filled with a great compassion as they watch their silent prayer.'

In Sledmere there is one particularly lasting memorial to Grandpapa. In Sir Tatton's copy of the Eleanor Cross which stands outside the walls of the house there are niched panels, and in each of these Grandpapa had set separate brasses in memory of his friends killed during the War. 'Ye who read this remember Edward Bagshawe, killed in Flanders, *Preux chevalier sans peur et sans reproche*; Walter Barker, a footman of Sledmere, and a private in the 5th Yorkshire Regiment; Harry Agar, an agriculturist and a Lance-Corporal, and a Sergeant, and many others, officers and men, who died with them.' By chance he had left one panel unfilled, and there his own figure was blazoned in the brass, armoured and sworded, a Paynim lying under his feet, for scroll the Laetare Jerusalem, and in the background the Holy City.

Grandpapa's funeral procession moving up the main street of Sledmere village.

Chapter 8
Papa, Uncles and Aunts

WHILE GREAT GRANDPAPA was living out his last years at Sledmere, from time to time he would send for his grandchildren to stay with him. They would arrive with their nannies and take up residence on the top floor of the house. All other floors and passages were out of bounds. Each morning they would be dressed up in their best clothes and led downstairs to the boudoir, a room off the main hall, to say good morning to their Grandfather. There he sat in state, his French companion, La Comtesse de Lichterveldy, by his side. The routine would always be the same. They would enter the room, shake his hand, say 'Good morning, Grandpapa', and leave, either for a walk in Sylvia's Grove, or back to the confines of the nursery. Until it was destroyed by fire, this was their total experience of Sledmere.

When Aunt Freya, Papa, Uncle Christopher, Aunt Petsy (Everilda) and Aunt Angela arrived from Eddlethorpe in 1915 to live in the newly rebuilt house they walked into a veritable children's paradise. No longer did they have to tread softly. This was now their own home without any restrictions on where they could or could not roam. Because the interior of the house was not quite completed they were temporarily housed in what was to be the servants' wing, but they lost no opportunity in taking advantage of the great spaces of the main building. Hide and seek was played all over the house, and soon the long downstairs passages rang with screams of terror as Aunt Petsy, blindfolded, was raced up and down at speed in an old wheelchair discovered by Papa. 'Rats and Ferrets', a game in which the Rats hunted the Ferrets and the Ferrets hunted the Rats, was played in pitch darkness in the Library, now stripped of all the paraphernalia of Jessica's day and more like it was when Great Great Grandpapa paced its length. Slowly but surely life was breathed into the new house.

The upbringing which their parents had given them meant that the one thing none of the children lacked was a powerful imagination. On their father's short and infrequent trips home he never failed to hold them all spellbound in every possible way, relating endless stories of his travels in far-off lands, often exaggerated into true-life *Arabian Nights* fantasies. There were also, remembers Uncle Christopher, 'passionate family excursions led by him to York and Beverley and to little known churches in the East Riding where there was a Norman Arch or a Saxon Font, or to some place where there was a ruin – it hardly mattered what – provided it dated from far beyond living memory'. There were other more

(left to right) Aunt Freya, Papa, Uncle Christopher, Aunt Petsy and Aunt Angela.

curious treats: 'He procured a copy of that most grotesque of English classics, *The Castle of Otranto* by Horace Walpole, and every evening when he could, he read us a chapter, accompanied by coloured illustrations of the more striking incidents made previously by himself. It was his romanticism again, this time taking a splendidly farcical turn. The pictures are of the kind that can make you laugh aloud, and I remember that he used to laugh aloud as he drew them . . . . Whenever he was at home we all seemed to be involved in a world of romance and excitement and laughter.'

Grandpapa also passed on to them the love of the macabre which he had inherited from Monty James. He never, when in Paris, missed an opportunity of visiting the Grand Guignol and on his returns home he loved to gather everyone round and recount blood-curdling tales of the terrifying plays he had seen. In fact, with the exception of Aunt Angela who was not then born, they had all undergone a true-life experience which was far more horrific than any of the tales he could tell, and which made them perhaps less frightened than they might otherwise have been.

While they were still living at Eddlethorpe, and while their parents were away, Nanny Duntz announced one morning that she was going to take them all on a special treat. What that treat turned out to be, Aunt Freya still remembers with horror.

We were all dressed up, and trooped out into the farmyard, which was the other side of the road. Here there was . . . well, I thought it looked like an altar, and a man standing by it in a white coat, and there were several large basins and bowls nearby, and knives and things. I suddenly realised what we were in for and I became absolutely petrified. Then two men dragged an enormous pink pig into the yard shrieking its head off. Richard immediately burst into tears and roared the place down. Lizzie Nicholson tried to control the twins, who were only two! Before our eyes a sort of hammer and chisel were placed in the middle of the pig's forehead. It was in this way stunned and fell down and at the same time its throat was cut from ear to ear. I have never seen so much blood in all my life. It was all collected in a basin. By that time I was pea-green in the face. I think that at that moment Lizzie protested and we were all taken away. Then I always remember at children's hour going down to tea where Grandmama Gorst was in charge. She was a very sweet old lady and she said, 'And what did you do this morning, dears?' and I blurted out, 'We saw the pigs killed!' Then there was the most awful rumpus. My parents returned that evening, and there was Nanny Duntz in tears and saying she was going to leave, and the whole house seemed upside down.

Nannies and children: (left to right) Marie Duntz, Freya, Richard and Lizzie Nicholson.
(opposite) One of Grandpapa's more macabre illustrations to Horace Walpole's 'The Castle of Otranto'.

The whole Sykes family photographed at Sledmere early in 1917, on one of Grandpapa's rare visits home. The baby sitting on Edith's knee is Daniel who was born in the summer of 1916. (opposite) Aunt Angela was a talented illustrator from an early age.

Left to themselves at Sledmere the children's imaginations ran riot. Papa and Uncle Christopher invented two Jekyll and Hyde characters called Mrs Clixon and Mrs Jugsisson whose identities they used to assume. Papa was Mrs Clixon, an evil witch who used to terrorise the younger ones. One day he came dangerously close to persuading Aunt Angela to leap into the depths of the septic tank. Indeed she would have done so had it not been for the timely appearance of the kindly Mrs Jugsisson. There was also a general obsession with the French Revolution, after a reading of *A Tale Of Two Cities*, and Papa, as was then possible, ordered the estate works yard to construct for him a miniature guillotine. As no one questioned the order this was duly built, perfect in every detail right down to a real blade. The morning it was delivered Papa assembled his brothers and sisters in the courtyard and proudly announced that he was going to demonstrate it. The chosen victim was, once again, poor Aunt Angela, and her head was actually laid beneath the blade before the others intervened. 'But it's only Angela,' protested Papa.

As in all big families there were quarrels among the children. Sometimes things got a little out of hand.
(opposite) Ghosts played a large part in everyday life.

When Grandmama discovered the truth about the guillotine's blade her fury knew no bounds. In the end however she relented about having the machine destroyed so long as the metal blade was replaced by a wooden one. When this alteration had been carried out the guillotine was removed to the cellars where it was to provide the centre-piece of a brilliant entertainment. The Sledmere cellars, like those of most large country houses, are large, dark and ghostly, and here the children combined their talents to create a gruesome world of fantasy. There were macabre tableaux of every kind. One depicted the horrors of the French Revolution with corpses and decapitated heads modelled by Aunt Angela, who was fast becoming an expert sculptress, and bloody slogans daubed all over the walls in red paint such as 'Vive la Revolution' and arrows pointing the way to 'Madame Guillotine'. In one corner a devil crouched ready to pounce on some unsuspecting victim. In another a huge spider, made by Aunt Freya, hung down from the ceiling. They left no dark place unhaunted by some monstrous face or dismembered limb, each strategically placed so that by the sudden light of a candle it would be revealed in all its ghastliness.

Each Christmas all their cousins used to come and stay, none of whom were spared the horrors of the cellars. There were favourite older relations too, such as Aunt Hylda, loved for her splendid looks – she had dyed black hair and was very made up – and her prowess at charades; and Uncle Harold, a charming wastrel who kept them all in fits of laughter. One of the highlights of Christmas was the Goose Pie, a speciality of the cook Mrs Matthews, which made the centre-piece of the cold-table. In appearance this was like a huge square pork pie with raised pastry. To make the pastry alone required twenty-four pounds of flour, six pounds of butter and half a pound of suet. The filling consisted of layer upon layer of boned game all wrapped around one another: on the outside was a goose, then a turkey, two ducks, two pheasants, a hare and six woodcock. It came to the table eight days after cooking in the large oven of the black coal range that dominated the kitchen.

Uncle Christopher, Aunt Freya, Aunt Petsy and Aunt Angela dressed for one of their plays.
(opposite) Father Dunstan Pozzi, a priest from the nearby monastery of Ampleforth,
on whose life Papa based the story of his film 'From Toe Dancing to Tonsure'.

As the children grew up, and after the death of their father, they abandoned none of their childhood fantasies. The only difference was that, now, instead of it being small cousins who were led unsuspecting into the cellars, it was their friends from London or Oxford and Cambridge. Their charades became Shakespeare plays or Greek tragedies performed in the grounds, while Papa, his eyes fixed firmly on Hollywood, saw himself as the Cecil B. de Mille of Sledmere, and wrote and directed a series of films. He called his production company 'Photo-Richard'.

Two of these epics have survived. The first is 'Flames of Desire', a story of brutal feudal oppression in which Sir Otto Brightmire, the evil landlord played with much relish by Papa, torments the pathetic Bugthorpes, a poverty-stricken peasant family, finally raping Florrie, the wife, before being murdered in an act of revenge by the husband. The second is the masterpiece 'From Toe Dancing to Tonsure', which tells the story of how Dunstano Pozzi, an Italian toedancer, is lifted from the obscurity of the streets of Naples when the king, Bomba, falls in love with his beautiful sister. After a series of mad adventures involving, among others, Garibaldi, Queen Mary and an American millionairess called Mrs Cory, he is finally driven to begging for asylum in the monastery of Ampleforth. Once again Papa takes the juiciest roles, those of the Abbot of Ampleforth and King Bomba of Naples. The main character Pozzi, played in the film by Uncle Christopher, was in fact based on a real Father Pozzi, an Ampleforth priest who had befriended the family and spent much of his time at Sledmere, where he was regarded as something of a joke figure by all the children. The completed film was shown to some of Pozzi's fellow monks who received it with howls of laughter, though Papa never dared show it to Pozzi himself.

In the early 1930s Uncle Christopher appeared in a film written by the American actress-novelist Elinor Glyn.
He was awarded the role because she believed that 'only gentlemen could play gentlemen'. It was, remembers Aunt Freya,
'without any doubt the worst film I have ever seen in my life'. In this scene from the film
Uncle Christopher shares the screen with fellow stars (left to right) Cyril Connolly, David Herbert and John Sutro.

Papa driving one of his early Rolls Royce motor cars. He had a reputation for fast driving
and on one occasion, when appearing in court for speeding, was described by the judge as
'a menace to mankind'. He had been travelling at forty m.p.h., 'a speed', said the judge, 'too terrifying to contemplate'.
(opposite) Papa with what his mother would have considered a group of 'fast young things', on holiday on the French Riviera in 1933.

Had Grandmama, a devout Catholic, survived long enough she would certainly not have been amused at the irreverence of 'From Toe Dancing to Tonsure' which included one scene of an orgy of drunkenness and gluttony involving the Abbot of Ampleforth and his monks. In fact she died in 1930 before the film was started. She did however witness with amusement the making of 'Flames Of Desire', and she also lived long enough to see a new era of 'bright young things' at Sledmere. During this period there was only one innovation to which she could never be reconciled, and that was the dreaded cocktail, then at the height of fashion. The reason for this was simply that most cocktails were made of gin; gin had been Jessica's favourite tipple, and Grandmama was terrified lest any of her children should go the same way. Cocktails were forbidden. When Papa brought his fast young friends home he was forced to find somewhere they could drink in secret, and in a room deep in the servants' wing he opened a sort of speakeasy. Here the bright young things would come to mix and sip the deadly mixtures: White Ladies, Bronxes and Sidecars were the specialities. Then one day in the midst of the cocktail hour, while the room was filled with the din of shaking ice, clinking glass and chatter, chatter, chatter, the door opened and in walked Grandmama. Those who could hid behind curtains; the rest stood helpless in deathly silence, as she froze the room with a look of utter scorn and walked out. It was a bad and never-to-be-forgotten moment.

Life at Sledmere continued as gaily as ever throughout the 1930s, the only noticeable difference being that now the cocktails were served in the drawing room. It became famous for its Sidecars and there was much jazz and dancing. At the end of the decade, of course, it all came to an end, but at least the house was never shut up. It was requisitioned as a hospital for troops and so remained full of life. In 1943 Papa married my mother, Virginia Gilliatt, and when, at the end of the war, they moved back into Sledmere, the whole cycle started again. It has never stopped.

Papa at the piano in the music room at Sledmere. He was a very talented jazz pianist, and contemporaries remember how, in the twenties and thirties, his playing was always a feature of gatherings.

(overleaf) Papa on a visit to China in the 1930s.
The giant elephant against which he is leaning is one of the stone guardians of the Ming tombs outside Peking.

Papa and Mama, Virginia Gilliatt, on their wedding day.